St. Anthony of Padua:

Wisdom for Today

St. Anthony of Padua: Wisdom for Today

By Patrick McCloskey, O.F.M.

Nihil Obstat:
>Rev. Lawrence Landini, O.F.M.
>Rev. Lawrence Mick

Imprimi Potest:
>Rev. Andrew Fox, O.F.M.
>Provincial

Imprimatur:
>+Daniel E. Pilarczyk, V.G.
>Archdiocese of Cincinnati
>August 16, 1976

The *Nihil Obstat* and *Imprimatur* are a declaration that a book or pamphlet is considered to be free from doctrinal or moral error. It is not implied that those who have granted the *Nihil Obstat* and *Imprimatur* agree with the contents, opinions, or statements expressed.

Photo credits: Salvator Fink, O.F.M., pp. 2, 12, 18, 113.
>Jack Wintz, O.F.M., p. 108.

Cover design by Michael Reynolds

SBN 0-912228-36-9

Contents

Repentance and Rebirth
Meditations for Lent and Easter

Virtues and Vices

The Church

Sacraments

Prayer

Mary/Meditations
for Advent and Christmas

Part III: St. Anthony Devotions and Prayers

The statue of
St. Anthony
above the main
door of his basilica
in Padua.

How to Use This Book

This book is divided into three unequal parts. In Part I, a short chapter on devotion to the saints is followed by an orientation to the 13th-century world of St. Anthony and a brief account of his life.

Part II consists of meditations on the words of St. Anthony. Each reflection begins with a quote from his sermon notes and ends with an application of his insight to the lives of modern-day Catholics. These are meant as prayer-starters, and need not be read in sequence. Topic headings have been added to help you choose a starting point for your prayer.

Part III contains explanations of the devotions connected with St. Anthony and a collection of the most traditional St. Anthony prayers.

St. Anthony was quick to acknowledge his debt to his Franciscan brothers who supported his sermons by their prayer and holy lives. As you read this book, please remember the Franciscans instrumental in its publication: Father Jeremy Harrington, who encouraged me to write about St. Anthony and then patiently edited the results; Father Ignatius Brady, who translated St. Anthony's quotes and who is an inspiration to any Franciscan; the friars who have advised me in the writing of these meditations. Naturally, I am also indebted to my family for more than I can say.

May this book draw you closer to God through the example of St. Anthony.

Today as when Anthony was a boy the towers of St. George Castle overlook Lisbon.

Part I: St. Anthony
and His Times

Devotion to the Saints

Why honor the saints, anyway? Unless we have a solid answer for that, our devotion to St. Anthony or to any other saint may be on shaky ground.

The saints remind us that the grace of God has not been fruitless. Holy men and women have generously cooperated with that grace in every era of history, on every continent, and in all walks of life.

According to Father Leonard Foley, saintly lives testify "that the Church *is* holy, can never stop being holy, is called to show the holiness of God by living the life of Christ." Furthermore, their holiness encourages *our* holiness, our attempts to live out the graced life we received at Baptism.

· We honor saints not to escape the demands of our lives but to receive from them needed inspiration.

What mother of a wandering child has not seen in Augustine's mother, St. Monica, an inspiration for her own prayers? Does not St. Joseph represent the holiness possible in very ordinary work and obedience to God? How many Christians working for the poor and the helpless have been encouraged by the work of Vincent de Paul and Frances Cabrini? Hasn't the example of martyrs strengthened Christians suffering persecution? Christ shows us the holiness possible in *his* situation; the saints show that same holiness in countless other circumstances.

We do not honor the saints because they can weasel something out of God that we cannot obtain by ourselves. Our motive is not that the saints possess some special skills that we lack. Rather, they have turned to God in prayer and encourage *us* to do the same. The second Eucharistic Prayer describes the saints as those who have done God's will throughout the ages. Their prayer for us helps *us* discover God's will and follow it.

The Church gives us the best of reasons for honoring the saints when at Mass it prays to God:

> You renew the Church in every age by raising up men and women outstanding in holiness, living witnesses of your unchanging love. They inspire us by their heroic lives, and help us by their constant prayers to be the living sign of your saving power.
>
> *Preface of Holy Men and Women I*

Another Preface proclaims:

> This great company of witnesses spurs us on to victory, to share their prize of everlasting glory, through Jesus Christ our Lord.
>
> *Preface of Holy Men and Women II*

Once there was a suspicion among Catholics that there were at least two "kinds" of holiness — one for priests and religious and the other for the rest of the people. Against this idea the bishops at Vatican II called one chapter of its document on the Church "The Call of the Whole Church to Holiness." The bishops wrote that the Church's holiness

> . . . is increasingly manifested, as it ought to be, through those fruits of grace that the Spirit produces in the faithful. It is expressed in multiple ways by those individuals who, in their walk of life, strive for the perfection of charity, and thereby help others to grow *(39)*.

There is only one holiness: God's. Lawyers and housewives and machinists can all be holy if they accept with faith their circumstances and duties in lif and "cooperate with the divine will by showing every man through their earthly activities the love with which God has loved the world" *(41)*. Ours is a universal Church: extended from Christ to the present, all over the world, speaking practically all languages, and encouraging men and women in countless different vocations to "live a life worthy of their calling" *(Eph 4:1)*.

Obviously, not all saints are canonized. Only 173 saints are celebrated in the Latin Rite Church. Even Butler's *Lives of the Saints* lists only 2,500. The real number is known to God alone. Surely each of us knows several saintly people. In honoring the canonized saints, we honor the most obvious examples of the one holiness that comes from God.

John Kennedy closed his book *Profiles in Courage* with a passage which is as applicable to holiness as it was to his subject:

In whatever arena of life one may meet the challenge of courage, whatever may be the sacrifices he faces if he follows his conscience — the loss of his friends, his fortune, his contentment, even the esteem of his fellow men — each man must decide for himself the course he will follow. The stories of past courage can define that ingredient — they can teach, they can offer hope, they can provide inspiration. But they cannot supply courage itself. For this each man must look into his own soul.

We do not always choose the exact circumstances of our lives, but God's holiness is possible wherever we find ourselves.

The World of St. Anthony

In what sort of world did Anthony live? Briefly answering that question from the political, religious and social viewpoints will help us identify with Anthony and the people he served.

Political. When Anthony was born in Portugal in 1195, it had been independent of two neighboring kingdoms, Leon and Castille, for only 56 years. The entire country had been placed under the Pope's protection in 1143; four years later the Moors were driven out of Lisbon. Only in the reign of Alfonso II (1211-23) did the quarrels between pope and king over rights of jurisdiction become really sharp.

Italy likewise was in political turmoil. Supposedly under the protection of the Holy Roman Emperor (now a German king), Italy saw many battles in the

12th and 13th centuries. Periodically, the emperor's troops would move south against rebellious city-communes in northern and central Italy. Papal troops, sometimes defending the Papal States in central Italy, were often allied with Italian groups against the emperor.

Men were still fighting in the Crusades. The fourth one ended in the sack of Constantinople (present-day Istanbul) in 1204, and the sixth one, led by Emperor Frederick II, resulted in a treaty (1229) giving access to the Holy Places.

In the late 12th and early 13th centuries, Italy split into pope and emperor factions which occasionally arranged truces but which never really settled their disputes. The Moslems continued to be considered a threat, especially when the emperor led Moslem troops from Sicily and southern Italy against the pope's army.

Religious. The late 12th and early 13th centuries were also times of great religious activity. Itinerant preachers, some approved by the Church and others censured by it, preached to the people in an emerging Italian vernacular. "Reform" was the current cry, for the wealth of the Church and the scandalous life of some clerics were undermining the Gospel message. To meet these changing needs, new forms of religious life arose, especially the mendicant followers of St. Dominic and St. Francis.

New heresies also arose. In southern France the Albigensians considered themselves the only Christians pure enough in thinking and way of life to be saved. Since they believed that the material world was created evil, they scorned marriage, the value of human life, holding property or belonging to a visible Church. In northern Italy a lay group called the Waldensees vowed themselves to poverty and preaching the Gospel. Eventually many of them became heretics, rejecting the Church and some of its sacraments.

Small wonder that Francis of Assisi and Dominic Guzman established religious orders noted for their commitment to the visible Church and its leader, the pope.

During this time two ecumenical councils were convoked (Lateran III in 1179 and Lateran IV in 1215) to aid the reform of the Church. During Anthony's lifetime three reforming popes, Innocent III, Honorius III, and Gregory IX, contributed their energies toward rooting out abuses.

Social. Amid the political and religious turmoil, there was also far-reaching social change. Feudalism, that centuries-old political-economic landholding system, was declining though its ideal of chivalrous knighthood was far from dead. More and more men and women were living as free people in the rapidly expanding cities. Coined money became more common and was displacing land as the real measure of wealth. The growing merchant class favored a city-state system of government. This led individual city-states into conflict with each other and with their legal ruler, either the Holy Roman Emperor or the pope.

Into this world and to men and women experiencing all these changes, Anthony came to preach the Gospel.

The Life of St. Anthony

Martin and Maria Bulhom were delighted at the birth of a son in 1195. When they baptized him Fernando at the cathedral church in Lisbon, Portugal, little could they suspect that this child would some day be known throughout the world by another name and in connection with a faraway city. Martin and Maria, members of the local nobility, sent Fernando to the nearby cathedral school for his early education.

At 15 he joined the Augustinian Canons at Sao Vincente monastery in Lisbon; however, this monastery was too close to Fernando's worldly friends and to the king's quarrels with the Church. Two years later Fernando was given permission to transfer to Santa Cruz monastery in Coimbra, a city 100 miles north of Lisbon. There he eagerly studied Sacred Scripture and the writings of the Church

VS SACRIS SERMONIBVS AVRES
VLAS PISCIS HABERE PROBAT

Fresco of St. Anthony preaching.

RGAT AB OMNI
VVS ADIRE PATREM

Fathers to prepare himself for priestly ordination. But this monastery was not always peaceful either, for its superior and the local bishop were involved in a dispute between King Alfonso II and Pope Honorius III. The Augustinians at Santa Cruz were understandably split into factions.

Fernando's path did not cross that of the followers of St. Francis until some of the first friars at Coimbra came to beg at the house of the Canons. Later, the bones of the first Franciscan martyrs were brought from Morocco to the Augustinian monastery in Coimbra. Inspired by such sacrifice, Fernando was captivated at the thought of martyrdom. Soon after when some friars came begging, he told them, "Dearest brothers, gladly will I take the habit of your Order if you will promise that as soon as I do so you will send me to the land of the Saracens, there to reap the same reward as your holy martyrs and gain a share in their glory."

In the summer of 1220 at the Coimbra friars' little house dedicated to St. Anthony the Abbot, Fernando received the Franciscan habit and took the name Anthony. Soon afterwards he was given permission to preach to the Moslems.

This missionary trip was one of Anthony's big disappointments, however. He became very sick in Morocco. In the spring of 1221 he sailed for Portugal.

On the way his ship was blown off course to Sicily where he spent two months recuperating with the friars. Then he went with them to the Pentecost Chapter (meeting) in Assisi. There he saw St. Francis. When the Chapter ended and the 3,000 friars prepared to return home, Anthony asked to join the friars working in northern Italy. Father Graziano, the superior, assigned him to the hermitage at Monto Paolo near Bologna; part of the time Anthony prayed and the rest of the time he cared for the needs of the other friars there. Cooking and washing dishes were part of Anthony's duties.

In the summer of 1222 Anthony attended the ordination of several friars. At the dinner afterwards, the superior asked one of the friars to preach. All the Dominicans and Franciscans present declined except Anthony who amazed the friars with a marvelous sermon on Christ's obedience, even to death on a cross. A hidden talent was revealed!

Anthony soon received permission to preach throughout northern Italy where heretics had recently won many followers. The Church's wealth was causing a bitter controversy, and the poor and simple lives of these wandering dissident preachers contrasted sharply with the lives of many priests and bishops. Anthony won converts by his sermons and by his simple way of living.

Soon Anthony received another job — teaching theology to the friars in Bologna. His previous studies in Coimbra served him well at this time. Anthony the teacher always heeded the command St. Francis addressed to him: This study of theology must not destroy the spirit of holy prayer and devotion. Indeed, Anthony's students learned Scripture from a man as holy as he was learned.

In 1224 Anthony was sent to southern France to preach the Gospel where the Albigensians had made many converts. There he earned the nickname "Hammer of Heretics." In fact, Anthony won over the dissidents as much by his holiness and great charity as by his learning. He said the preacher should, by word and example, be a sun to his listeners. "The sun is the source of light and of warmth: a symbol of our life and our teaching.... Like two streams, these must overflow from us to men; our light must warm the hearts of men, while our teaching enlightens them."

Once at a national meeting in Bourges, Anthony in the midst of his sermon turned to the archbishop and said, "Now I have something to say to you who wear the miter!" He then encouraged the archbishop to root out the evil in his own life. In France, Anthony again taught the friars Scripture and served as superior in two places.

In 1227 Anthony returned to northern Italy where he was made provincial (head) of the friars in that area. He continued his popular preaching. Only in 1228 did Anthony come to Padua where he immediately won over the people. At this time he wrote down his Sunday sermons — actually sermon notes to aid other preachers. Two years later at the request of Pope Gregory IX, he wrote down his sermons on the saints.

Despite all his preaching, Anthony always made time to pray, especially at La Verna, the favorite retreat of St. Francis.

At his own request in 1230, Anthony was relieved of his job as provincial. He returned to Padua where his Lenten sermons the next year drew thousands daily; no church was large enough to hold the people. Confessors, including Anthony, were busy after these sermons. Anthony's preaching persuaded Padua to pass a law against the then commonly accepted practice of imprisoning debtors until they paid off the complete debt. Anthony also preached against charging very high interest for loans; rates of 25-30 per cent were then legal in Padua.

Not all of Anthony's efforts were blessed with success. In 1231 he failed to bring peace between two warring political factions in nearby Verona.

In the spring of 1231 Anthony withdrew with his companions, Brother Luke and Brother Roger, to the friary at Camposampiero where he had a sort of treehouse built as a hermitage. There he prayed and prepared himself for death.

On June 13, 1231, he became very ill and asked to be taken back to Padua. On the way, at the friary in Arcella, Anthony received the last sacraments. Shortly before he died, he called out, "I see my Lord."

Immediately a dispute arose over Anthony's burial place. Citizens from Padua naturally wanted him buried in their city; the citizens of Capo di Ponte also claimed that honor. The Poor Clares, cloistered nuns following the Rule of Francis' friend Clare, wanted Anthony buried in their monastery, near which he died. After the podesta (mayor) of Padua asked the men of Capo di Ponte to come and discuss the matter with him, he jailed them while the bishop of Padua conducted the burial of Anthony in the friars' church in Padua.

Anthony had not been dead a month when the people of Padua petitioned Gregory IX to enroll Anthony among the saints. A commission of cardinals investigated Anthony's life and the miracles offered as indications of his holiness. Of the 46 miracles approved for Anthony's canonization, only one was worked in his lifetime. On May 30, 1232, in a packed cathedral at Spoleto, Gregory IX proclaimed Anthony a saint and assigned June 13 as his feast day.

When Gregory later announced this canonization

to the whole world, he wrote: "To be considered a
saint by those who belong to the Church Militant, two
things are necessary: namely, virtues and miracles.
These must mutually bear witness to each other, since
neither merits without miracles nor miracles without
merits fully suffice to prove to men the holiness of
anyone. But when genuine virtues precede and
evident miracles follow, we possess sure signs of
holiness which induce us to venerate him whom God
by such merits and signs bids us honor."

Already before his death, the Paduans had
referred to Anthony simply as "the Saint." Pope Leo
XIII called him "the Saint of the world," and in 1946
Pope Pius XII declared him a Doctor of the Church.

In the same year that Anthony was canonized, the
people of Padua began building a basilica in his
honor. In 1263 this church was completed enough to
allow his bones to be transferred there. St.
Bonaventure, head of all the Franciscans in the world,
was present for the transfer, and when he saw that
Anthony's tongue alone had remained intact, he cried
out: "O blessed tongue, you have always praised the
Lord and led others to praise him! Now we can clearly
see how great indeed have been your merits before
God!" In 1350 Anthony's bones were transferred to a
chapel within that basilica. At his tomb there, millions
of pilgrims have prayed asking his help.

The cloister in the monastery in Coimbra where
Anthony lived as an Augustinian

Part II: St. Anthony's
Words for Today

The Challenge: Living in the World

"The world is like a field, and to bear fruit there is
as difficult as it is praiseworthy. The hermits bloom in
solitary places and shun the company of men. The
monks blossom in a garden enclosed and hide
themselves from the eyes of men. How much more
glorious is it if a Christian brings forth fruit in an open
field, the world, for all too easily the twin sprouts of
grace — the spirit of a life of virtue and the fragrance
of a good name — wither there and die."

When Anthony says that bearing fruit in the world
is difficult, he tells us nothing new. More important is
the encouragement he offers to lay men and women
whose vocation is "in the world." That's where most
Christians live out their baptismal faith.

One problem is immediately obvious. "The
world" and we ourselves often conspire against a
virtuous life, against our attempts to follow Christ.
When gospel standards oppose the practices of the
world, we too often make the wrong choice on the
basis of comfort.

"The world" — should we despise it or imitate it?
Our spiritual life depends on how we answer this
question. If we totally reject our time in history and
our society, are we really Christ's disciples? But on
the other hand, if we take our values and blueprint for
living from the world around us, how can we claim to
be living out our baptismal promise to follow Christ?

Reflecting these questions, Vatican II's
Constitution on the Church described the spirituality of
lay men and women: "They live in the ordinary
circumstances of family and social life, from which

the very web of their existence is woven. They are
called there by God so that by exercising their proper
function and being led by the spirit of the gospel they
can work for the sanctification of the world from
within, in the manner of leaven. In this way they can
make Christ known to others, especially by the
testimony of a life resplendent in faith, hope and
charity."

"A life shining in faith, hope and charity"
modernizes Anthony's terminology of "bearing fruit."
Those who desire to act as leaven in society recognize
both that it needs a Christlike witness and that as part
of God's creation it is worth saving. Somewhere
between bitterly condemning the world and aping its
ways, all Christians must find the proper soil to root
themselves and so fulfill their earthly responsibilities
and grow spiritually. Then monks and hermits will
bloom or wither in their proper place, and lay men
and women in the open field will either succumb to
what is evil in the world or overcome it by faith, hope
and charity.

The Spirit as Fire

"The power of fire overcomes all things and is not
itself subdued; it imparts its action to the things it
encompasses, renews everything that comes near it,
and does not decrease as it spreads itself. So too does
the Holy Spirit pervade all things by his power, for he
is ineffable in his might. When he enters a soul, he
fills it with his fire and lets it enkindle others. All
things that draw near him feel his renewing warmth.

21

He leads all hearts upward to heaven."

Anthony is not exactly original in comparing the
Holy Spirit to fire; the Acts of the Apostles used the
image of tongues of fire to describe Pentecost. But
why this connection anyway?

Perhaps Anthony serves us best in pointing out
that when the Holy Spirit enters a soul, he fills it with
fire and allows it to enkindle others. At Baptism we
were anointed as a mark of our reception into the
Christian community and into the life of the Trinity.
At Confirmation we were anointed in the form of a
cross and received the fullness of the Holy Spirit to
strengthen us in our life with God. The gifts of the
Holy Spirit (wisdom, fortitude and the other five)
were given as aids to keep us faithful to the life of
grace we had begun and which God seeks for us. The
fire enkindled in us at Baptism and Confirmation was
meant to remain and to grow as we live more and
more after Christ's example. Through contrition and
penance the fire is again enkindled.

Yet the fire has not always grown in us. Many
people have received the Holy Spirit in Baptism and
Confirmation and have allowed that spark to grow
cold through unrepented sin. Even worse, instead of
enkindling others, Christians sometimes extinguish
any traces of the Spirit's life. Hearts once enthusiastic
over life with God sometimes grow stone cold and
scandalize others.

Why? Many reasons might be offered, but one
reason may be the root. Though the Spirit gives many
gifts, one is clearly superior: charity, the enduring
love God has for us and which we in turn show to our

brothers and sisters and to ourselves. God offers his grace and enkindles our hearts, but he never forces us to respond; that would violate his respect for us. Thus, we determine whether we persevere in charity and radiate the warmth of the Spirit's fire or show the coldness of our own selfishness. And according to our decision, others will be drawn to knowing God or will be sidetracked. Scripture says, "A brother helped by a brother is a strong fortress" (Prv 18:19). Can we afford to work against the grace of the Spirit?

Bearing Fruit in the Spirit

"When it is cold, the leaves drop off the tree and one looks in vain for fruit; a proof that warmth is the good and nourishment, so to speak, of all living things. In us, that warmth is the grace of the Holy Spirit. When it is lacking the heart of a man grows cold and ceases to bear fruit, and soon the frost of sin destroys all the life that was in him. 'Wisdom will not abide in a person that is in debt to sin' (Wis 1:4). When vice enters, virtue leaves!"

Values — everyone is talking about them these days: the values that shaped America, the values of Catholicism, which values have priority, how to resolve conflicts of values and especially how to transmit values from person to person, generation to generation.

Gospel values receive their warmth, their ability to grow, from the grace of the Holy Spirit. Grace enables gospel values (such as charity and hope) to grow in surprising places even under very difficult circumstances. The saints show the great variety of people and situations in which gospel values can take life. And American Catholics have shown that diversity also. St. Elizabeth Seton's work was not exactly like Father Junipero Serra's labors, but both showed gospel values founded on Jesus and his grace. Such diversity is still alive in U.S. Catholicism.

As American Catholics join with Catholics worldwide to renew Catholicism (i.e., to follow Jesus more faithfully and continue his work), we should remember the central role of grace. Any renewal of externals without a comparable determination to cooperate with God's grace will produce an inverted pyramid bound to topple. But if you and I plus the rest of American Catholics seek the Lord in greater purity of heart and with more generosity in responding, then the renewal of gospel values will be firmly rooted in God and will bear fruit.

A tree without warmth carries no leaves and produces no fruit. We who follow Jesus can ignore the place of grace and go it alone — fruitlessly — or we can welcome the grace of God and our need for it — and so become fruitful.

Grace as Sunlight

"God's mercy rebukes the sinner even as the Lord chides Job. 'Have you any inkling of which is the way to the home of light or where darkness lives?' (Jb 38: 18-19). That light is grace and darkness is the blindness that fills the soul of the sinner. How

desperately we need that light to see the sad state of
our conscience! Look! When it is dark, we do not see
how dusty and dirty our house is. Only when the
place is flooded with sunlight do we realize its awful
condition. So we need the light of God's grace to show
us the real state or our soul and induce us to clean up
our hearts!''

Anthony's comparison of light to grace and
darkness to sin is rather common in Scripture.

God, says Genesis, is the source of all light.
Sometimes he reveals himself in connection with light
(e.g., Moses and the burning bush, the pillar of fire at
the Exodus). The Servant of Yahweh is a light to the
nations, a messenger of salvation (Is 42:6).

The light imagery is continued in the New
Testament. Jesus is the true light that enlightens all
people (Jn 1:9) so that whoever believes in him need
not stay in darkness any longer (Jn 12:46). Indeed,
Christ's followers are to be a light for the world
(Mt 5:14-16).

On the other hand, Satan is called the prince of
darkness, yet he would have us believe that following
him is the way to enlightenment. Adam and Eve did
not consider being as wise as God — the consequence
of eating the forbidden fruit — a deed of darkness;
however, it was exactly that. It is no accident that this
prince of darkness is also called the father of lies. He
promises light and freedom but delivers only
darkness and slavery. Thus, the apostle Paul told his
followers to expose the deeds of darkness by the
contrast of their lives (Eph 5:8). They were to be a
light shining in the midst of a twisted and corrupt
generation (Phil 2:15).

How shall we remain children of the light? We must follow the words of Jesus as they are given in Scripture and understood by his followers, the Church. We must initiate the example of his saints — past and present. And we must be willing to squint a little as the price of leaving the darkness.

The light of Jesus is a challenge to us. In its presence we can open up and see our need to repent again and do so, or we can close up more tightly and hope the light will go away. Christ's light can brighten the darker corners of our soul — if we allow it close enough.

Preferring darkness, however, is still a possibility

Sainthood: Blooming Where You're Planted

"The saints are like the stars. In his providence Christ conceals them in a hidden place that they may not shine before others when they might wish to do so. Yet they are always ready to exchange the quiet of contemplation for the works of mercy as soon as they perceive in their heart the invitation of Christ."

Anthony reminds us that holiness is not meant for the believer's self-esteem but for building up the Body of Christ. Saints do not show their holiness completely on their own terms "when they might wish to do so." No, they move into public notice only "on the invitation of Christ."

Of the 173 saints mentioned by name in the

Missal, the largest single group is that of martyrs (49).
And we can safely assume that the majority of them
would just as soon have died naturally, strong in their
faith, as suffer publicly for witnessing to Jesus. But a
quiet end was not their call. On the other hand, we
know of saints eager to risk their lives in faraway
missionary work but who were not called to it. Such
was Anthony of Padua's first ambition as a
Franciscan.

God's holiness is not merely for the benefit of the
individual saint. These are to shine "like the stars" for
all God's people. Not all the saints are well-known
(e.g., St. Pancras), yet they still build up the holiness
of Christ's Body. In fact, the majority of persons who
now enjoy the sight of God are not formally
canonized. And each of us probably knows several
saintly people who will never have that title officially.

That individual men and women are holy is
important for the whole Body of Christ. They
strengthen it by silently yet forcefully testifying that
God's grace has been sufficient and fruitful in
countless situations, spread over many lands and
centuries. Even though we honor saints long dead, we
do not suggest that presently God's grace has found
no cooperative recipients. The age of holy men and
women has not passed us by.

Do we need the saints? Yes — to pray for us and to
remind us that holiness is possible for all believers in
every age. But the greatest canonized saints cannot
provide a walking, talking, flesh-and-blood example
of God's holiness for the people who know us. That is
ours to do, and their holiness can never substitute for
our own.

Devotion to the saints can either encourage

sanctity in us or provide an excuse for laziness. Will our light be bright with God's grace or dull with our own self-satisfaction?

Imitating Saints: How and Why

"The stonemason and the bricklayer are careful to use the measuring line, a pendulum and bob, to make sure the walls are straight. Can't we say that the virtuous lives of the saints are like a measuring line stretched over our souls to make sure our lives take the proper shape and measure up to their good example? Whenever, then, we celebrate the feast of a saint, let us look to them as giving us the pattern our lives should take."

Anthony's comparison is eye-catching, but we need to ask *how* the saints are to be the pattern for our lives.

If we take Anthony's expression too literally and try to imitate the physical details of a saint's life, we will surely get off on the wrong road to holiness. Francis of Assisi, for example, once had a follower who tagged after him and imitated his every move, even coughing. "Stand on your own" was Francis' advice.

Another error is to think that it's impossible to really imitate a saint like Anthony or Francis because we live in a world quite different from theirs. But Francis did not complain that he did not live at the time of St. Benedict. Maria Goretti did not moan that she lived much later than St. Clare. Nor did the other saints waste their time wishing they lived closer to earlier saints. Each one has his or her own work to do. And the grace of God which supports this work is still plentiful.

The holiness of Joseph is not imitated by becoming a carpenter. Nor is the sanctity of Elizabeth Seton copied simply by becoming a teacher. The saints are not a measuring line for us in that literal sense.

Most of them differed from each other in occupation, historical situation, education and personal outlook. What then did they have in common? Together, what can they tell us about holiness?

Each of them says God alone is the source of every good and must be praised. Each of them made the Gospel the basis of his or her life. And each of them surely followed both of the two great commandments.

To many Christians today Mother Teresa of Calcutta is a saint. Does she want to restrict holiness to imitating her life's work? No. "Holiness," she says, "is nothing more than accepting Christ and living his life in us. It means doing his will, whatever he wants." Her eyes are on Jesus and everything else is judged in relation to him.

And that is how the saints can be a measuring line for us: They remind us to reorder our lives in relation to Jesus. Without this, imitating the life of Mother Teresa — or any of the saints — becomes empty, without any core. But because their eyes are on Christ, the saints encourage us to put ours there too.

Sharing Joys and Burdens:
A Saintly Activity

"Each saint in heaven rejoices over the glorification of the other, and his love overflows to him. . . . The same joy will fill all the blessed, for I shall rejoice over your well-being as though it were my own, and you will rejoice over mine as though it were yours. To use an example: See, we are standing together, and I have a rose in my hand. The rose is mine, and yet you no less than I rejoice in its beauty and its perfume. So shall it be in eternal life: My glory shall be your consolation and exultation, and yours shall be mine."

In very personal terms, Anthony describes the harmony which the saints enjoy. They are so quick to join in the good fortune of each other, very prompt to appreciate a beautiful, fragrant rose, yet slow to covet it.

At death the saints do not suddenly learn to share in each other's glory. No, they continue the mutual support which they practiced in this life. They carry on their attitude of not growing bitter and jealous over the talents and good fortune of others. Why? There is no need to be envious: God is mindful of what he gave you and only expects to be praised through those gifts. Also, the talents of others aid all of us through building up the Body of Christ. Jealousy destroys this common work.

Just as the saints while on earth rejoiced over each other's gifts, they also fulfilled St. Paul's advice to "bear one another's burdens and so you will fulfill the law of Christ" (Gal 6:2). Surely the following of Christ is a sharing in both the joys and the sorrows of other believers. And perhaps the saints rejoice because they know how to share both the glory and the suffering of each other. After all, isn't there something shallow about sharing only the good times of your friends?

Jesus said, "This is how all will know you are my disciples: your love for one another" (Jn 13:35). Christians know, of course, that this love comes from God's grace and not from their own strength.

Two gardeners standing side by side can enjoy a beautiful rose because both of them know that for all their hard work, they cannot make a final claim for its beauty. So also, two followers of Jesus can overcome any temptation to envy the good they see in one another because they realize that only God is the ultimate source of goodness in this life. And so they can praise God's works wherever they are found.

Because of their common Father, the saints in heaven give each other joy and consolation. If we intend on following Jesus and thus someday joining them, we need learn to do likewise.

Giving Our All

" 'You shall love the Lord your God with your whole heart.' Note well that Christ says: your whole heart! He doesn't leave a corner of your heart for yourself, but bids you offer the whole to him! He bought the whole of you by giving his whole self for you, that he alone might possess every part of you! Do not try, like Ananias and Sapphira, to hold back any part of yourself, or else like them you will lose all! If

31

you really wish to have the whole, then give it all to him, and he will give you all of himself; and thus you will have nothing of yourself — and yet will have him and yourself besides!"

If Anthony's words sound like a riddle — if you want to be whole, give yourself totally to Christ who gives himself completely for you — consider how you would describe your relation to Christ. When Anthony says that if we give ourselves to Christ we will have nothing of ourselves and yet have Christ and ourselves besides, he is not talking nonsense.

When we try to give ourselves totally to Christ — that is, to follow his way to the Father and so to other people — we are living out our Baptism, turning more and more from sin and the "empty works" of the devil and trying to keep bright our baptismal faith and innocence (symbolized by the baptismal candle and cloth). Giving God our "all" means sharing in Christ's death and resurrection.

But as we grow older we realize two things about ourselves and Christ: 1) The "all" we give to Christ changes as we grow. At 25 it isn't exactly the same as it was at 15, or will be at 65. 2) We cannot give ourselves totally to Christ in one grand moment and never have to reconfirm it. Anthony certainly realized that as time passed God expected him to be more and more generous in giving up selfishness, false pride, old grudges and whatever else he might like to keep for his own comfort and out of God's sight. Giving God last year's "all" could not be enough. But, we say, life would be so much simpler if only we could dedicate ourselves entirely to God's way just once and be done with all this "every day" business. Indeed,

Baptism does join us to Christ permanently, yet it also begins a process which requires a follow-through in our daily living.

Christ would be easier to follow if giving our "all" required always the same love and sacrifice under favorable conditions, or if we could live off a single gift of self to God without having to renew it again and again. But would that be the Good News we have received from Jesus?

Practicing Humble Service

" 'You must befriend one another, as Christ has befriended you, to the honor of God' (Rom 15:7). See indeed how Christ became a friend of all! He received the blind, to give them light; the lame, to make them walk; the lepers, to cleanse them; the deaf, to restore their hearing; the dead, to give them new life; the poor, that he might preach the Good News to them. So must we befriend one another! If your neighbor is blinded by pride, give him light as far as you can by your humility. If he is afflicted with the leprosy of sin, cleanse him by the word and example of a holy life. If he is deaf from avarice, set before him the example of the poverty of Christ. If he is dead from gluttony and drunkenness, your abstinence may help restore him to life. In this way the poor themselves in turn preach the Gospel and the life of Christ to others."

These words of Anthony alert us to a basic principle of Christian life. If we hope to follow Jesus, then this friendly concern for all people "to the honor of God" must characterize our lives.

Yes, we may say, but aren't there enough people helping the needy already: government, Churches, charitable groups and individuals? Do they need my help too? In this passage, Anthony does not mention the material needs of people — he expected his listeners would make adequate provision for them. In our day that presumption may not bear up so well and may require extra action of us. But Anthony here cites man's spiritual needs: blinded by pride, diseased from sin, deaf from avarice, and dead from gluttony and drunkenness. And these spiritual weaknesses are no respecters of status.

Yes, but what can I do? For a start, open your eyes (or keep them open!) and see these needs when they are close, as they often are. Perhaps you don't know anyone suffering from gluttony, but what of the deadly sins of pride and avarice? Have they disappeared in our century? And if I do see such a need, what then? Insofar as possible try to offer corresponding help — not out of haughty superiority but humbly as one who might some day need this same aid, as one who may yet need to hear this same Gospel message and to see it active in a fellow Christian's life.

Humble service "to the honor of God" can be a part of our life if we make it so. Anthony says it is worth the bother.

Feeding Christ in His Poor

"Today Christ stands at our door and knocks in the person of his poor. It is to him that we open when we give aid, when we give ourselves to those in need; for he tells us plainly, 'When you did this to one of the least of these brothers of mine, you did it to me'" (Mt 25:40).

Remember, says Anthony, that in aiding a needy person you are giving to Christ himself. Yes, but there are so many poor families in the U.S. and in the Third World who lack food, others who lack no material goods but hunger for spiritual aid, and still others who need a word of encouragement or simply a minute of my time. Because of God's wondrous plan, the Incarnation, all these people in some way represent Christ to me. Yet how can I help them all?

I cannot. If I gave away all my money, there would still be poor people in the world. But I should not let this paralyze me. Rather, I should start by doing what is possible for me, by helping the poor people I actually know or meet.

Then I should count on the help of many men and women of good will who are also concerned about helping the poor. According to my means, I can give to others who I know are aiding the unfortunate.

And money is not the only thing necessary. Together we can take steps to help change sinful structures and systems that make and keep people poor.

But when it comes to satisfying a hunger for spiritual aid or encouragement, we are not limited by our financial means. If we offer support to a friend who is depressed, we do not lose anything except time. A kind word to a stranger is not so costly, and a visit to a friend or relative in a nursing home will not bankrupt us. No, these take only our time and good will — and an eye ready to see people in need.

Matthew 25 records that the virtuous and the wicked asked the very same question: "Lord, when did we see you as a stranger or hungry, thirsty, naked or sick?" The virtuous did not think of themselves as aiding Christ, nor did the wicked see Christ in the people they rejected.

But God has come among men in Jesus and restored them to his image. "The second commandment is like the first," says Christ. And so we read, "If a man who was rich enough in this world's goods saw that one of his brothers was in need, but closed his heart to him, how could the love of God be living in him?" (1 Jn 3:17). Christ does not ask us to offer financial and spiritual assistance to the needy so that we can feel satisfied with ourselves for a job well done. No, we offer it to persons who in some way represent Christ to us and are thereby our redeemers.

As Instruments of God's Grace

"When a crystal is touched or struck by the rays of the sun, it gives forth brilliant sparks of light. When the man of faith is touched by the light of God's grace, he too must give forth sparks of light in his good words and deeds, and so bring God's light to others."

Thus Anthony illustrates how a simple example from nature can sometimes demonstrate a great religious truth. The man of faith, he says, is like a crystal which reflects the rays of the sun. The crystal is important, but it is not the source of its light; it reflects the sun's light. When the man of faith is touched by God's grace, he shows this grace to those around him through his life. Such a person knows he is not a source of grace but rather an instrument of it.

Being an instrument of God's grace to others is no small job. The crystal which is chipped or covered with dirt cannot reflect the sun's light as it should. Thus we are deprived of seeing a distinctive part of the sun's light. The follower of Christ who is scarred by indifference toward God or his neighbor or who is dulled by obstinacy in sin cannot reflect the grace and love of God as well as the alert and penitent Christian.

Do my good works make me more worthy or deserving of God's grace? Because I visit a friend, donate money to the United Fund or light a votive candle, does God "owe" me anything? No. Does that mean I am wasting my time in these and similar activities? No. Any "good work" is worthwhile if done as a result of faith in God and gratitude for his mercy and grace. Good works become "bad works" when carried out in a bargaining way, as if God is now under contract to the doer. Good works are not guarantees that God will prevent suffering from coming to us, for example. They are not a means to anything — except the praise of God. Truly good works are performed humbly and in thanksgiving for God's goodness.

St. James tells us that faith without good works is

dead (2:26). The story of the Pharisee and the tax collector praying in the Temple (Lk 18:9-14) tells us that good works cannot substitute for faith. Both must work together.

The crystal brings brilliant sparks of light to places which would otherwise be darker. We, too, may be the only way some people will experience today the love and grace of God. Can we afford to lose that opportunity?

St. Anthony's Example: A Meditation on His Feastday

"O the mercy of God! Never does he refuse to be merciful but is ever present to those who turn to him, as Isaiah says: 'Cry and the Lord will answer; call and he will say: I am here, for I the Lord your God am merciful' " (Is 58:9).

Anthony had good reason to appreciate God's constant mercy, for he experienced it personally and saw it active in the lives of others. How else could he explain his own Franciscan vocation and the religious conversions that he inspired in others?

Surely God's mercy and goodness encouraged Anthony to leave his monastery and become a Franciscan missionary, for he hoped to imitate the friars who had recently been martyred in Morocco. But a storm drove Anthony's boat instead to Sicily and from there he joined a group of friars in Italy. When his preaching ability was recognized, he was sent to preach to fallen-away Catholics, to spark the faith which had grown cold in them. Convincing people that God had not abandoned them was his life's work.

Anthony's famous preaching brought thousands to hear him praise God and invite his listeners to repent, to turn their hearts to God. Sometimes he defended the Catholic faith against error through his sermons. More often he gave moral exhortations about daily living, the type of sermon St. Francis loved so well. The quote above was probably the basis of such a sermon. Whether Anthony preached to hardened sinners or to pious but sinful Catholics, he stressed that God was always ready to forgive the sinner.

Why was Anthony so successful in leading men to God in his own day? Why is he still so successful today? His listeners knew him as a prayerful man who personally felt the mercy and goodness of God. We find in Anthony the encouragement for our own turning more fully towards God; we see him as a man faithful to his call to follow Christ and we take courage that with God's grace we can do the same.

In June we celebrate Anthony's feast. While most of us are not called to the public preaching which made Anthony famous, we can ponder the great mercy and faithfulness of God and gradually open our hearts even more to him. Then, we will be helping others who do not realize how generous our Father is. Our example can be a sermon. In fact, Anthony credited the success of his work to the prayers and example of his brothers who preached not verbally but with their lives. Example is no less powerful in the 20th century.

Seeking the Desert

"When God proposed through the prophet Hosea
to bring back to himself his faithless spouse Israel, he
promised: 'I will allure her, I will lead her into the
desert and speak to her heart.' Does not God do the
same to the erring soul that he wishes to draw to
himself? At the beginning he allures us by his grace,
enlightening our hearts and inspiring us to grow in
virtue. Then he leads us away from sin and vice and
idle thoughts into the desert, to inner solitude, to
peace of mind and heart. Finally, when one becomes
strong in virtue, he speaks to our hearts in the depths
of prayer."

Anthony's love for Scripture is obvious from this
quote. For he recalls a powerful Old Testament scene
in which Hosea's faithless wife is used as a symbol of
Israel. God's plan is to lead Israel back into the desert
(figuratively) and there speak to her heart, recalling
her previous love for God alone and inviting her to
repentance. Israel, says God, has gone after many
other lovers, but there is still hope if she will
recognize her error and return to her Lord.

But why the desert? For Hosea and for Anthony it
represented a fitting setting for God to invite a whole
nation or individual sinners back to faith in him. In
the desert there are fewer distractions, and amid its
barrenness God can again show that he is the Lord
who brought Israel out of Egypt and who has brought
us, through Jesus, to redemption. In the desert, a
person is more likely to hear God's voice and
remember his goodness.

God intends, says Anthony, that the erring soul be

given this chance to repent in the desert, to show a change of heart. And so God offers his grace to encourage us to reflect on our sins and to see them apart from their usually attractive surroundings. With this peace of heart we can again hear God's voice within our hearts. And we can respond in grateful prayer.

But the desert is also a frightening place, both physically and spiritually. For we do not like to face that we have wandered from God's way. And we fear that part of ourselves we may meet in solitude. Furthermore, the desert accents our dependence on God and is a reminder that we cannot bring ourselves out of sin into freedom. After all, it was God who led Israel into the desert. He alone fed the people and gave them water, and he alone brought them across the Jordan into the Promised Land. He can act that wondrously again for us if we let him, if we allow ourselves to be called into the desert.

With God's grace and our cooperation, the desert can be for us a place of rebirth and new fruitfulness. Or it can remain frighteningly sterile.

The Call to Repentance

"The sinner who has recovered the grace which he had lost has three reasons for being full of joy. He should rejoice that he did not die in his sins and face everlasting punishment. He should be glad because he has been restored to God's favor though he merited it not. He should rejoice that he will be brought to glory if he perseveres in his new-found friendship.

Let him then sing with Isaiah, 'I exult for joy in the Lord; in my God is the joy of my soul' (61:10)."

Much of Anthony's preaching, as the quote above shows, was directed to inviting sinners to repentance, to stressing the urgency of interior renewal and to working as Francis of Assisi did at reconciling men and women to their Creator and to the rest of creation.

Pope Paul once said: "This renewal and reconciliation pertain in the first place to the interior life, above all because it is in the depths of the heart that there exists the root of all good and, unfortunately, of all evil. It is in the depths of the heart therefore that there must take place conversion or *metanoia*, a change of direction, of attitude, of option, of one's way of life." In all this Anthony would wholeheartedly agree.

Conversion occurs in the depths of the heart. Anthony would understand that. After all, he said that the repentant sinner "will be brought to glory if he perseveres in his new-found friendship." Perseverance, fidelity — beautiful ideals but oh the cost! Changing the direction of one's life is no small matter. But a solid change there has a magnified effect. For example, Pope Paul has said: "Repentance, the purification of the heart and conversion to God must consequently bring about an increase in the apostolic activities of the Church." Inner conversion will burst out in a greater urgency to spread the Good News about Jesus, most especially through lives which bear the fruit of the Gospel and "give reason for the hope that is in us" (1 Pt 3:15).

So what is God now asking of us? To weigh again how much we let the Gospel affect us, to consider

anew how we as individuals and as a Church spread
the Gospel. Is it taking root in our lives?

The work before us is great and our time is short.
But with God's grace and our cooperation, we can
make good use of this opportunity.

Facing Our Sins

"The sinner must unhesitatingly put all his works
squarely before his mind's eye and regard them often
and attentively with sorrow of heart. In this way he
will be able to produce from them the fruit of
penance. Were one courageously to set his inner self
before his eyes, he would find nothing there but
reason for true sorrow of heart and the desire to
return to the ways of God."

For all his preaching of repentance, Anthony was
not a morbid man. He simply knew that we ought to
recognize and confess our sins rather than deny or
ignore them.

Anthony knew what he was talking about. Years
of public preaching to fervent and lapsed Catholics
and private counseling made him very familiar with
unrepented sin. What then does he advise? That the
sinner "unhesitatingly" put all his works "squarely"
in mind and regard them "often and attentively" with
sorrow of heart.

Unhesitatingly — we may not be eager to change
our ways, but then we have not repented until we
consider our sins without hesitation. *Squarely* — we
do not convert until we give our own sins a direct and

hard look. *Often* — not so that we immobilize ourselves through scrupulosity, but frequently enough to remember that we are sinners. *Attentively* — this helps our intention to accept God's grace and resist this sin when the occasion arises again.

If the sinner does all this, says Anthony, he will have reason enough for "true sorrow of heart and the desire to return to the ways of God."

Where, then, is the difficulty of repenting? "Hardness of heart" was the Old Testament description which Anthony surely knew. During the Exodus, the ancient Israelites sometimes grumbled that God had brought them out of Egypt only to have them starve in the desert. Concerning one such incident over the water supply, God warns: "Do not harden your hearts as at Meribah, as you did that day at Massah in the wilderness, when your ancestors challenged me, although they had seen what I could do" (Ps 95:8-9). Similarly, we harden our hearts when we refuse to see any sin in our lives, when we persistently avoid looking at the effects of our actions and omissions.

Medically we know that the hardening of our arteries restricts the flow of blood and our full functioning. Likewise, we know that there is a spiritual "hardness of heart" which rejects God's grace and shuns all opportunities for repentance. If we are honest with ourselves, we can with God's help overcome this spiritual affliction.

Examining Our Conscience

"When a house is shut up, the sun's rays do not enter, and so we don't see how much dust is found therein. But when the sun's rays penetrate, we soon realize how full of dust the house is. Self-knowledge is just such a ray, since if the sinner but pause and reflect, he will see how marred and tarnished is his conscience, and be conscious how much dust and dirt his darkened soul had concealed."

When Anthony compares a dusty house to a soul darkened with sin, we follow that easily enough. The exposure of dust by the sun is also easy to see. But what is this self-knowledge that activates the conscience and lights up our sins?

When Jesus was on this earth, he provoked men and women either to close themselves off from his saving message (some of the Jews) or to receive him and so repent and believe the Good News (other Jews). Peter's first plea to Christ was "Leave me, Lord. I am a sinful man" (Lk 5:8). Zacchaeus, a dishonest tax-collector, changed his life on meeting Jesus (Lk 19:8-10). When the Samaritan woman came to know Christ, she too was converted (Jn 4). Some people, however, met Jesus and closed themselves off — for example, many disciples left Jesus in disbelief after his teaching about the Eucharist (Jn 6:66).

Jesus brings us to self-knowledge. He helps us understand that we are capable of sin and do sin, but that if we turn our lives more and more toward God, we can be healed by the effects of Christ's life and death. We understand that before God all men are sinners who have been saved by his grace and ought to live worthily of that redeemed condition. Sometimes we fail to do so, and thus dust and dirt accumulate. But if we ignore our sins and say there is no dust, then our consciences become dull and we are less able even to recognize the dust.

Anthony says that if the sinner will pause and reflect, he will see how tarnished his conscience is. It is helpful for us to meditate on how Jesus brought men and women to decision about their lives. The more we know Jesus, his message and his redeeming work, the more we know ourselves and where we need to ask forgiveness. But if we gloss over the Gospel and apply it to everyone but ourselves, then we have ignored the decision and the self-knowledge that meeting Jesus can mean.

Self-knowledge is not always a picnic for us; It can hurt to admit our sinfulness. But for the followers of Christ there is no alternative. If we block out the light, dusty rooms get worse and become more unlivable.

God's Mercy

"O the mercy of God! Never does he refuse to be merciful, but is ever present to those who turn to him, according to the word of Isaiah: 'Cry and the Lord will answer. Call and he will say: I am here, for I the Lord your God am merciful' (Is 58:9)."

Anthony appreciated the mercy of God and often preached about it. Indeed, this mercy is at the heart of all Scripture.

In the Old Testament God constantly acts with

mercy; he is faithful to Israel because his will to save
that nation does not change. Whatever mercy men
and women may show palely reflects the mercy that
God exercises for his chosen ones. God's faithful love
(mercy) is the root of his revelation.

When the ancient Hebrews wanted to summarize
God's loving care for his people, they composed
Psalm 136 which begins, "Let us praise the Lord for he
is good, for his mercy endures forever." This psalm
continues by citing 25 examples of God's faithful love
— each answered by the refrain "for his mercy
endures forever."

When God sent prophets to Israel, they warned
that imitating God's mercy is more important than
offering Temple sacrifices. "It is mercy that I desire,
not sacrifice, and knowledge of God rather than
holocausts" (Hos 6:6). The mercy of God is so
encompassing that, as Jonah found out, even pagans
who repent will be spared.

In the New Testament the mercy of God is always
before us. Luke's Gospel is sometimes called the
Gospel of Divine Mercy because Jesus is so often
receiving repentant sinners (e.g., the penitent woman
or Zaccheus) or telling parables about them (the Great
Supper, the Prodigal Son). Matthew's Gospel tells of a
servant who was forgiven a huge debt yet later
refused to forgive a lesser debt owed to him (Mt 18:
21-35). On that occasion Jesus presents the Father as
merciful *except* to people who refuse to pass on to
others the mercy they have received.

Even in his hour of greatest suffering, Jesus asks
mercy for those who crucified him. And when the
apostles hurry out after Pentecost to preach the Good

News, the mercy of God is central to their message. Paul's preaching is rooted in God's mercy, for in Romans we read: "It is precisely in this that God proves his love for us: that while we were still sinners, Christ died for us" (5:7-8).

Anthony certainly realized that some people can't imagine that God's mercy is generous enough to pardon *their* sins. Therefore, they do not repent or offer these sins for forgiveness. God is merciful: we can count on that. Yet he will not pry sins away from us in order to forgive them.

God's Judgment

"God gives his judgment to the just man, the good follower of Christ, that he may judge himself, so that God will not find anything in him to condemn. 'If we judged ourselves,' says St. Paul (1 Cor 11:31), 'we should not be thus judged.' Give me your judgment, O God, that I may make it mine and making it mine may escape yours!"

These words of Anthony recall that God's judgment on all of us aids salvation — if we learn from it. Otherwise the judgment is indeed a fearful thing. But if God judges us not only at the end of time but now, how do we experience this judgment?

Our everyday living provides some occasions. For example, we may repeat a story about someone only later to find out the story was false and the person's reputation has been damaged. As we try to undo the harm, who hasn't seen here the judgment of God?

When we reflect on our lives, who cannot identify several times when God's judgment was evident?

This judgment often comes to us through other people; for example, from the honest criticism of a friend. Perhaps this is part of God's constant love for us — that someone will offer us this service and this opportunity to start anew.

The judgment may come to us from an organization or a group of people such as Christ's Church which leads us closer to God and to our brothers here on earth. Yet how can that happen if no one ever points out the obstacles to love of God and love of neighbor? It cannot, and so this corrective ministry is an important part of the Church. The pope, bishops, pastors and all members are called to offer correction with charity when necessary. In this way we are forewarned of our sins and have an opportunity to turn our hearts back to God.

Anthony was a great student of Scripture; surely he remembered that in the Old Testament God often judged his people and invited them to greater faithfulness to his way. Though many rejected these prophetic messages, God never gave up on his people. "I will not turn around and destroy Israel; for I am God and not a man, the Holy One in your midst," says God in Hosea 11:9. God corrects us when necessary but he never forces his way on us.

Anthony asks us to search out God's judgment in our lives and make it our own, to measure ourselves against his will and try to follow it. In prayer and confession we have two aids for this task. In this way a constant search for God's judgment will not leave us surprised on the final day.

Obstacles to the Spirit of Penance

" 'My sacrifice, O God, is a contrite spirit' (Ps 50:19). The spirit of penance and contrition of heart, which as a breath of new life God breathes into the sinful soul of man, his image and likeness defiled by sin, becomes in turn a sacrifice the humbled sinner may offer to God to obtain pardon and reconciliation. For 'a heart contrite and humbled, O God, you will not spurn.' "

Anthony tells us that the spirit of penance is like a breath of new life, for the sinner may offer this contrition to God and obtain reconciliation. That sounds simple enough. Why do we find it so difficult to practice?

The greatest obstacle to a contrite heart is admitting that we have sinned, that we have in some way broken our relationship with God and with one another. We refuse to confess that we have defiled God's image by our sinfulness, and we do not like to think that God's trust in us and love for us was poorly placed. And so we prefer to deny our sinful actions. A stubborn heart will always be far from contrition.

A second obstacle to a contrite heart is the temptation to lose all confidence in God and in ourselves once we have acknowledged our sinfulness. Having fallen already in sin, we often prefer to think that God does not even care if we return to him. "I'm just no good," complains the hardened sinner. Getting up and starting out anew to our Father — as the Prodigal Son did — is very difficult even if we know he is waiting and looking for us.

The spirit of penance has yet another obstacle. No matter how hard the sinner tries, he cannot save himself; he cannot turn from sin without admitting that it is God who saves us. No amount of good works can replace that truth. Our role is not trivial — God will not save us against our will — but it is indeed secondary to God's great mercy and love.

If pride is the source of all sinfulness, as Anthony has affirmed already, then our difficulty in achieving a contrite, penitent spirit is obvious. Pride tells us not to admit we were wrong, not to start anew (and leave ourselves vulnerable to future falls), and to deny that we cannot "earn" salvation by our good deeds. On the contrary, a contrite heart admits sins, prepares to begin again to serve God and is quick to acknowledge that God's mercy and love are beyond anything we could ever imagine.

What can the sinner offer God? Not much, but then Anthony tells us that all God wants is a humble and contrite heart. Whether or not we receive that breath of new life depends on us.

The Cross: The Only Way to Glory

"Before his passion, Christ told the apostles: 'Now I am going to him who sent me.' Let us boldly ask Christ by what way he is going to the Father; and he will answer us: by the way of the cross, for the 'Christ had to suffer these things before entering into his glory' (Lk 24:26). Because he was man, he had labor and sorrow; because he was God, joy and eternal glory. Do we who follow him think we can have the one without the other? We must go the way of the cross too if we want to enter into the glory of Christ."

Anthony knew, as these words show, that Good Friday and Easter are meaningless without each other. Christ's way to the Father in glory was through an obedient death on the cross.

The dark hours come for everyone — in the form of sickness or tension or abandonment by those we love or temptation or discouragement with evil in and around us. These sufferings are our Good Friday, but to see that requires faith.

In looking back to Christ's time, we take the Resurrection for granted. It is hard for us to put ourselves in the position of the first followers of Jesus. What were the feelings of the disciples as they scattered for their lives? Wasn't the same faith required of our Blessed Mother on Calvary as at Bethlehem and at Cana?

Our temptation is to think that faith was very easy then but now difficult for us who never saw Jesus in person. The apostles would be surprised at that suggestion. For reliance on the faithfulness of God to his plan was as important then as it is now. Without the Resurrection the Gospel would not move us as it does and the grief of Good Friday would be unbearable. Indeed, that first Pentecost it was the Resurrection that gave Peter courage to proclaim that God had made this Jesus who was crucified "both Lord and Christ" (Acts 2:36).

On the other hand, without Good Friday what would we celebrate at Easter? Jesus rising — from what? His victory — over what? Christ **died** that all of us might be saved. St. Paul writes that Jesus "emptied himself" in becoming a man and humbled himself "to accepting death, even death on a cross" (Phil 2:6-8). Our Easter alleluias should be all the louder because of our belief in Good Friday.

We who hope to follow Jesus in his Resurrection cannot expect to skip over the cross. Anthony tells us what he himself learned from the Church: that Jesus suffered, died, was buried and was raised up in glory by the Father. We Christians cannot expect to improve on that sequence.

Our Role in Salvation

"The Lord says: 'I thirst for the salvation of man.' To what did he hasten? To the cross. Hurry after him then and carry your cross for your own salvation, as he carried his cross for your redemption! 'Whoever will follow me,' he says, 'let him deny himself by renouncing his own will and daily carry his cross by mortifying his body and follow me.' "

In this excerpt from one of Anthony's sermons, we face two worthy questions: How are we saved? What part do we play in God's plan for our salvation?

Yes, how are we saved? By the birth, life, passion, death and resurrection of Jesus Christ. God freely became man so that fallen man might see his Lord and know how loving a Father he has. Through the Scriptures, the lives of Jesus' followers and the Church, we in later days can experience and share this gift of Jesus. But sharing this, we can also expect to share the cross which Jesus knew and accepted.

Does God's plan for our salvation give us an insignificant, passive role? That depends on what we mean by passive. We are unable to heal the wound of original sin, to make good the sin of Adam. Christ alone died for that reason and was raised to life by the Father who wills that all men come to share the blessed life with him. Like the king who gave a feast for his son's wedding (Mt 22:1-14), God has prepared a great supper. However, he knows that love is not forced. The invited guests cannot be compelled to come. Nor are their reasons challenged. In this way we are active and share in salvation: We do not set the banquet, but we decide whether we shall accept our Father's generosity or tend to other "more important" business.

And so in following Jesus, we meet our cross. Surprised? Christ told us that his disciples must daily take up their cross and follow him (Mt 16:24). Before doing this we must patiently deny some of our inclinations — not because this mortification is great fun but because it may be necessary to align our attitudes with Gospel values. Crying "Lord, Lord" will not substitute for doing the Father's will (Mt 7:21). If the cross surprises us, perhaps we have forgotten what it felt like.

The Old Testament psalmist knew that "in no way can a man redeem himself, or pay his own ransom to God. Too high is the price to redeem one's life; he would never have enough to remain alive always and not see destruction" (Ps 49:7). We cannot save ourselves. However, neither can we sup at God's banquet if we ignore his invitation and think we can follow his Son in everything but the cross.

The Agony of Jesus

"When Jesus came in sight of Jerusalem, he shed tears over it (Lk 19:41). Yet the Lord wept not so much for the earthly city, but for the souls of its inhabitants: he lamented not the coming ruin of its houses, but the lives of its citizens. O Christian soul, if you could but see what is to come, perhaps you too would weep over your own life! But because you do not see, you do not weep, and perhaps are caught up in the vanities of earthly happiness which can only lead to everlasting affliction."

In his usual way, Anthony quickly gets to the basics: Jesus wept for those who, despite his suffering and death, would condemn themselves to live forever without God.

When I was in grade school, I learned that the greatest cause of Christ's suffering in the garden of Gethsemane was the thought that some people would choose to renounce their share in the salvation won on the cross. Dying for sinners was difficult enough; knowing that some would still choose against salvation made Jesus' vocation even more difficult. Now I am sure that part of Jesus' agony in Gethsemane resulted from natural human fear, but I still believe he suffered more from knowing that some people would be lost to God in spite of his death on the cross.

Perhaps this seems a strange beginning for an Easter meditation. But if St. Paul is correct in saying that Christ saved us by *obedience* to the Father (Rom 5:19), then we must follow that same path if we are someday to live forever with God.

55

More and more people currently believe that hell is really an impossibility, that regardless of how one lives salvation is guaranteed to each person. "God would not let someone go to hell" runs this line of thinking. If so, then what did Jesus mean when he said: "Not everyone who says to me 'Lord, Lord' will enter the kingdom of heaven, but he who does the will of my Father in heaven" (Mt 7:21)? If each person is necessarily saved, why did our Lord tell so many parables about living so as to be prepared always for the coming of the Master?

Anthony believed in the possibility of damnation. He did not particularly dwell on it or present it as the basic motivation behind the faithful following of Jesus. Indeed, hell cannot be that. It is simply the reminder that God takes very seriously the exercise of our God-given freedom to cooperate with him or to reject him.

Easter marks the victory of God's kingdom over the forces of evil. But we will share in that triumph only if we, too, are willing to follow the path of obedience — even when that path leads to the cross. Perhaps our Lenten penance will teach us how to walk as "children of the light" (Eph 5:8, 1 Jn 1:7) and to make those hard decisions which inevitably accompany a faithful following of Jesus.

Preparing for Easter

" 'Christ our Passover has been sacrificed' (1 Cor 5:7). On this Easter festival, then, let us celebrate our Passover meal, eating with bitter herbs the Lamb roasted for us on the spit of the cross and offered in sacrifice to the Father that mankind might be reconciled to him. Like true Israelites, we must celebrate the true Passover, with our loins girt in mortification and self-denial, our feet shod with the sandals of pilgrims, and the staff of good works in our hands, that in the end we may pass over with Christ Jesus from this world to the Father."

Anthony reminds us that Jesus came to lead all men to the Father. Preparation for this is important. Before the Israelites fled from Egypt, Moses told his people to celebrate a special Passover festival for their deliverance (Ex 12). Like pilgrims, with sandals on their feet and staff in hand, they were to eat unleavened bread and bitter herbs. This same feast Jesus celebrated on Holy Thursday. The perfect victim had not yet been offered.

Every year we too observe the feast of our deliverance from sin and death. We set aside 40 days to prepare for this, the great mystery of our faith. The Holy Week liturgy recalls Christ's passion and death and climaxes in the Easter Vigil's retelling of God's redemptive plan from Adam to Christ.

Yet sometimes we ask ourselves at Easter, where did Lent go? Once the Church ordered fasting as a single penance for its adult members. Now the Church prescribes it for Ash Wednesday and Good Friday and asks us to choose sacrifices more appropriate to our lives. Perhaps you have substituted some charitable work such as visiting the sick as your own preparation for Easter. Maybe you are looking for some other self-denial to replace fasting. What about working on whatever keeps you from God and your brothers — perhaps a quick and harsh tongue, begrudging forgiveness or neglect of family duties? More prayer, reflection or reading from Scripture are also important, for God wants inner conversion first and only then external penance.

Our Lord told several parables about being vigilant and ready for his coming (e.g., the wise and foolish virgins in chapter 25 of Matthew). By self-denial, charitable works and a contrite heart we can be ready, says Anthony, for Jesus' passing to the Father. Of course, if we are as ill-prepared as the foolish virgins, Easter will catch us by surprise.

Pride: The Root of All Sin

"As the body and all its parts are supported by the feet, so all vices are based on pride; for pride is the source of every sin."

Anthony says pride is at the bottom of every sin, but he doesn't explain why. What connects pride, for example, to denying God, stealing or malicious gossip? How can Anthony say all vices are based on pride?

When the originator of the Genesis story wanted to describe how man separated himself from God, he chose pride as the basis of his account. So that they could become God's equals, Adam and Eve disobeyed God's command. But by this action they disrupted the order which God had put into the world. The sin of pride separated them from God and brought division between Adam and Eve also.

Many non-Christians have also seen pride as the root of all sin. Ancient Greek mythology is filled with stories of men who wanted equality with the gods and were punished for it. Socrates' famous advice, "Know thyself," is really a caution against pride; the person who truly knows himself sees his strengths and weaknesses and is not likely to exaggerate either.

Pride usually threatens a person's balance in life by suggesting he is more important or talented than he really is. Sometimes it works in reverse. The person who continually denies his real talents is suffering the effects of pride also. Rather than risk failure, he prefers to excuse himself by downplaying his abilities.

Denying God, stealing, malicious gossip — what have these to do with pride? In each case a person disrupts creation because he does not value his own place in this world in relation to God and his fellowman. The two great commandments are to love God and love your neighbor as yourself (Mt 22: 36-40). Pride is an obstacle to both of these, for the man who is puffed up with self-importance before God (e.g., the Pharisee in the Temple) will not treat his neighbor justly. Likewise, the man who, to prove his own worth, humiliates his neighbor dishonors God.

If pride is the root of all sin, then efforts to counteract it will have good side effects elsewhere. The danger in pride is great, but then so are the benefits for bringing it into check. Anthony suggests the time to start is *now*.

Greed: Losing Control

"The avaricious man is really not rich, but poor. He does not control his money, but is controlled by it. He does not possess his wealth, but is possesed by it. He may have many things, yet for him he has all too little."

In these words Anthony shows us why avarice is self-defeating — no matter how many things a person feels he must seek and acquire, he is progressively more disappointed at having so little. The truly avaricious man, the miser, is perpetually dissatisfied. A person driven by greed cannot rest while there is something he does not yet control, and yet he is unhappy because the final control of his actions is now beyond himself.

Probably very few people are truly misers or totally warped by a lust for money and the material goods that money can buy. This disease, however, does not have to reach this extreme form to cause damage. A teen makes demands on a strained family budget for expensive stereo equipment. Is he a miser? Not really, not yet — but the same greed is operating in the teen as in the man who burdens the family budget by excessive credit buying.

Wait a minute! Is it wrong to own a car, to provide a house for one's family, to see one's grandchildren, to take a vacation and enjoy the world God has created? Certainly not, but each person must ask himself what the desire for money is doing to the priorities in his life. Gaining wealth might allow someone to do many good things, but it could also ruin the reason for seeking the money. The man driven to provide more and more things for his family may destroy the family through neglect in the process. The woman who pushes her husband to provide luxuries may be the eventual loser.

We as followers of Christ must not scorn the material goods which God created, but neither can we allow these goods to control us and separate us from God's love. This too would contradict God's creation. The Christian is not to neglect his own real needs, but he must be able to separate real needs from imagined ones.

The book of Proverbs tells us, "Better a little with fear of the Lord than a great fortune with anxiety" (15:16). Perhaps a person can have both wealth and reverence for God. But if the treasure threatens a person's love for God and for his neighbor (as it does in the case of a truly greedy individual), then the Christian knows which one to choose.

Hypocrisy: A Lamp Without Oil

"A good work done without devotion of heart is like a lamp without oil."

Isn't Anthony's imagery remarkable? So briefly he sums up a major problem for religious people: that their good works may be an empty shell containing no inner devotion, no true conversion to God.

Twenty centuries before Anthony, the prophet Isaiah denounced this same evil and recorded God as saying: "Trample my courts no more! Bring no more worthless offerings; your incense is loathsome to me.

New moon and Sabbath, calling of assemblies,
octaves with wickedness; these I cannot bear. Your
new moons and festivals I detest; they weigh me
down, I tire of the load. When you spread out your
hands, I close my eyes to you; though you pray the
more, I will not listen. Your hands are full of blood!
Wash yourselves clean! Put away your misdeeds from
before my eyes; cease doing evil; learn to do good.
Make justice your aim; redress the wronged, hear the
orphan's plea, defend the widdow" (1:13-17).

As such, the festivals and Sabbaths were not bad.
Only when celebrated without inner devotion did
they anger God.

The prophet Amos echoes this plea: "Hear this,
you who trample upon the needy and destroy the poor
of the land! 'When will the new moon be over,' you
ask, 'that we may sell our grain, and the Sabbath, that
we may display our wheat? We will diminish the
epha, add to the shekel, and fix our scales for
cheating! We will buy the lowly man for a pair of
sandals; even the refuse of the wheat we will sell!'"
(8:4-6). Such feasts will be turned into mourning, says
the Lord.

In the Old Testament, God commanded many
things of the Jewish people, but he always expected
them to *interiorize* the festivals they observed, the laws
they obeyed and the way of life he set out. External
observance of God's commands with no inner
devotion always borders on blasphemy, on mocking
God.

This problem of formalism was very much alive in
Jesus' time. Indeed, it was the basis for his
condemning the Pharisees. They performed many
"good works" even beyond what the Law of Moses

St. Anthony and the Child Jesus by Murillo.

required, but these works were not based on a deepening conversion to God's way. "Whitened sepulchers" was Jesus' description of them.

But the tragic sin of the Pharisees is still a possibility for us. We too can be outwardly devout yet all the while scheming against what we glibly profess. We too can perform our good works, being more concerned that we be applauded than that God be praised and served.

If you have a lamp without oil, you have two choices: either throw out the lamp or get some oil.

Overcoming Adversity

"It is only in adversity that we come to know whether we have made real progress in goodness."

What kind of man was Anthony that he would say something like this? Did he really love suffering? Did he seek it out? I doubt it, but he did not always figure it came from the devil either. *Sometimes* adversity comes because we are trying to follow the Gospel.

Perhaps when he spoke those words Anthony had in mind the admonition of Francis of Assisi: "We can never tell how patient or humble a person is when everything is going well with him. But when those who should cooperate with him do the exact opposite then we can tell. A person has as much patience and humility as he has then, and no more." Adversity can show us — by our reaction to it — just how much we are following Jesus and Gospel values.

In a sense adversity is ambiguous, that is, once it

occurs it does not automatically dictate a single long-term reaction. After the initial shock of a snide remark, for example, one person may retaliate in kind and keep the hurt alive while another victim may forgive and allow a painful memory to be healed by kindness. Job and his wife had very different reactions to the same disaster. She urged him to curse God; he refused.

In speaking of adversity Anthony is not thinking of sickness, natural disaster such as fire or flood, or man-made tragedy such as murder. Though we can have various reactions to them, I think Anthony was more likely referring to the kind of adversity encountered "in the line of duty" of our Christian living. If, for example, we really try to be peacemakers (Mt 5:9) and are opposed, then we are experiencing the sort of adversity Anthony and Francis mentioned.

And both of these saints knew such adversity. Francis sought to follow what he saw as the Gospel way of life, but some people considered him dangerous. The opposition he met from cynical heretics was easier to take than the lack of cooperation he received from some of his followers. Anthony also met adversity as he preached the Gospel. Francis and Anthony could have stopped that kind of adversity, but they were unwilling to leave the Gospel path to do so.

When you and I experience some adversity because of the Gospel, we are often so busy proving we have been unjustly treated that we do not notice our response may be more unchristian than the treatment we have just received!

Suffering is not a positive good for us to seek. But when it comes, we have some freedom in reacting to it. Which reaction we choose can tell us something about the extent of our Gospel conversion — if we listen to ourselves.

Charity and Humility: The Key Virtues

"Two things the devil fears above all: the fire of charity and the well-trodden path of humility."

This saying of Anthony is not immediately self-evident. Why did he give these two virtues special mention? Together what do they form? It seems that they show a person where he stands before God: weakened by original sin and personal sin but able because of God's grace to love God and his creation. Anthony here clearly echoes Francis of Assisi.

Humility is the great leveler of people, for as Francis realized, a person is no more and no less than he is before God. Such an outlook makes it harder to deceive either ourselves or others about our weaknesses and abilities. Thus Francis warned his followers to be courteous and humble as they go about in the world. Preaching was to build up people spiritually, not the ego of the preacher. In Francis's opinion, the Gospel cannot be lived in haughtiness.

Anthony, therefore, advises his listeners to make humility a habit, a "well-trodden path." People have reason enough to be humble — not denying their abilities but referring them to their Source — if they are willing to be honest.

But what of charity? It is humility's corollary virtue, the flip side of the coin, so to speak. If I admit that I am not perfect in God's sight, then I ought to be a trifle slower to lash out at the sinfulness in others, to tear them apart as if they alone fail to live as God's sons and daughters. Rather, humility and charity should prompt me to see the good in others and to call out the best in people (God's graced life).

Humility did not keep Francis from correcting his brothers when they strayed from the Gospel nor did it make him timid in announcing the Good News to all whom he met. But in both cases the great charity in Francis was important to the message and helped lead men to God.

If charity is not my basic orientation in living out the Gospel, then my witness stands very close to self-righteousness, to deforming Christ's image instead of spreading it. Without humility, however, my charity cannot be real.

Charity's solid root is humility; without it charity tends toward whimsical generosity to be doled out or withheld at my convenience — in other words, paternalism. Charity without humility was the mistake of those Pharisees condemned by Jesus. St. Paul, on the other hand, described charity as always patient and kind and never jealous or selfish (1 Cor 13:1-13).

Anthony was right: The devil has good reason to fear a charitable and humble person.

Poverty of Spirit/Purity of Heart

"The poor of Jesus Christ, who are marked with
the sign of his poverty as long as they are in this
world, consider themselves pilgrims and exiled from
the Lord (2 Cor 5:6) and walk roughshod over the
passing things of this world. Unless we keep our
hearts thus unfettered, how can we come to the
Lord?"

Christ asks us to be single-hearted, that is, to be
poor in spirit and pure of heart — all for the sake of
better knowing and loving God. When Anthony asks
us, "How can we come to the Lord unless we keep our
heart unfettered?," he perfectly describes this poverty
of spirit. What things bind up our heart?

Anthony answers this question in a general way
by saying we must be like the poor of Christ who
consider themselves as people always on the move
towards God and thus give little attention to the
passing things of this world. The poor of Christ do this
in response to the Gospel (e.g., lilies of the field story).

Yet Christ's call seems contradictory. We are to be
pilgrims always on the road to God, but we are not to
despise the world in which we live. Pilgrims too must
be concerned about dying lakes, substandard schools
for blacks and undernourished children in Brazil. We
are not to be overly concerned with our fame or
fortune, yet we are not merely "marking time" here
on earth with our surroundings as our chief obstacle
to God. Those who are single-hearted must try to
work out a way of being pilgrims without being
irresponsible to those with whom we share this life, of

being concerned with the things of this life yet not enslaved by them.

More personally we can ask what keeps our hearts from the Lord? For some it is greed; for others it is uncontrolled ambition. An all-consuming pride keeps some people from God, while the relentless pursuit of pleasure is the downfall of others. In 1,001 ways we estrange ourselves from God, and very often each of us has a unique way of doing this. Often this rejection of God shows itself in our turning away from our fellow human beings.

Anthony is telling us to be poor in spirit, to unfetter our hearts and free ourselves to love the Lord and live accordingly. Each must respond according to his own situation and loosen the shackles — whatever they may be — that keep him from God. The task is hard, but heaven's gate is only wide enough for those willing to begin this anew each day.

Gaining or Losing Faith and Charity

"There is no greater sorrow in the world than that of a mother whom death has robbed of an only and much-beloved child. So there should not be any greater sorrow than that of the penitent soul which has lost by mortal sin its only son, that is, 'faith which works through charity' (Gal 5:6). Charity is the soul of faith and gives it life and energy; but if we lose charity by sin, faith itself must die within us."

Anthony used powerful examples as these words show. But isn't his comparison of the death of an only child and the loss of faith overdramatic? How important is charity to faith?

The soul can lose its only son (faith) through mortal sin. Sometimes we talk as though that could happen every day of the week. But can this sin be entered into and repented of so quickly and so often? Or truthfully, isn't mortal sin really built on a *series* of actions and attitudes so that at some particular crisis point we may choose to reject God. Is mortal sin all that sudden and surprising? Or isn't it really the end-product of carefully nourished attitudes? A person may for years nurse along racial prejudice until someday he explodes in very unchristian action.

How does the soul lose "faith which works through charity"? We backbite here, are selfish there; and eventually cutting corners with God becomes a pattern, a way of life. "God surely won't mind if I . . . ," we say. Then we often include the very thing which separates us from God.

The soul does not lose or gain faith and charity in isolated moments. Whether we like it or not, our attitude and action today towards God and his world is influenced (for good or bad) by how we were yesterday. And this in turn influences how we will be tomorrow. Charity is the power from God to shape ourselves gradually more in his likeness than we were yesterday. If we give up on charity, our devotion to God collapses.

"A chain is only as strong as its weakest link," we say. If charity, then, is the basic orientation of our lives, by God's grace our links will stand under great stress.

When a mother grieves over an only child's death,

she knows her tears can never restore the child to life — but grieve she must. The soul which has lost faith and charity can, however, in grief beg God's forgiveness and receive new life. But in this God made the first step long ago; the next step is ours.

Gospel Living: Doing the Father's Will

"To say 'Lord, Lord' in the right sense (Mt 7:21) means to believe with our heart, praise God with our lips, and bear witness to him by our deeds. If one of these is lacking, we are not confessing but denying God; if our life belies our belief, it counts nothing to shout God's praises."

Again, Anthony knew what he was talking about, for nothing dampens faith quite so quickly as a verbally pious person whose actions tell a conflicting story. This must have been a complaint in the time of Anthony. It certainly was in Christ's day and remains so in our own.

But why all the fuss anyway? Christ has said, "It is not those who say to me 'Lord, Lord' who will enter the kingdom of heaven, but the person who does the will of my Father in heaven" (Mt 7:21). Doing the will of the Father — that will offset any temptation to be a quick and easy believer, full of nice phrases but short on living out the Gospel. Holiness is not a matter of who talks best but who lives out completely the faith he professes with his lips. Talk is so often cheap. But

71

Gospel living which includes the cross is never cheap.

Why do some people find it difficult to believe in Jesus? Are they simply stubbornly denying what they know is true? Are they stupid? Not likely. Perhaps they have never gotten over the discrepancy between Christian promise and Christian performance. These people are not playing games. Indeed, they often very carefully compare the conduct of Christians to the claims of Christians, and conclude that since the conduct is not inspiring, then the whole thing is false.

Paul the Apostle mentioned this same thing in his letter to the Romans. He said that if a Jew boasts of having the Law of Moses and then fails to keep it, "you bring God into contempt. As Scripture says: 'It is your fault that the name of God is blasphemed among the pagans' " (Rom 2:23-24). Similarly, the atheism in our time is sometimes fueled by the way Christians live.

Sin will always represent the gap between what we profess and how we live. But as long as we are trying to make our words and actions sing the same tune, then we are on the right path. What Christ and Anthony both feared was the person who would never even notice that his smooth-talking faith stood in contrast to his way of living.

Christ has called on all his followers to be "doers of the Word" and not hearers only. Please pray that priests will match Gospel promise with performance — by God's grace — and will lead other believers to do the same.

The Church:
Built and Guided by Love

"As the tiller keeps the ship on its course and brings it safely to port, so must love of our brothers in Christ guide the community of the faithful and keep them on the right path and so bring them at last to harbor. For where charity and mutual love are found, there is the community of the saints of God."

Once again Anthony's image quickly catches our attention. But is it true that our love for Christ's followers keeps the Church on the right course?

Jesus' Last Supper instructions suggest that: "This is my commandment: love one another as I have loved you. A man can have no greater love than to lay down his life for his friends" (Jn 15:12-13). Only by exception are Christians asked to lay down their lives physically for the sake of Jesus' followers. But Our Lord clearly suggests that if he could make that total sacrifice for us, we can sacrifice ourselves for our brothers and sisters in the faith.

And love for the community has its tests. One day the sinfulness of all the Church's members may depress us. Another day we may find a single follower of Jesus who doesn't look very lovable. Not passing God's final judgment on some people can indeed be a cross for us.

But love for the community can also keep our following of Jesus real. St. Paul told the Galatians: "My brothers, you were called, as you know, to liberty; but be careful, or the liberty will provide an opening for self-indulgence. Serve one another, rather, in works of love, since the whole Law is summarized in a single command: 'Love your neighbor as yourself.' If you go snapping at each other and tearing each other to pieces, you had better watch or you will destroy the whole community" (Gal 5: 13-14).

"Tearing each other to pieces" — don't we know how easy that can be? Sniping at the character of this person, harping on the admitted faults of another, planting an innuendo in an eager ear — are these so difficult to imagine or find among the followers of Jesus? Large-scale religious wars among Christians have died out in most places, but too many Christians are carrying on their own private wars. That Jesus gave us *two* great commandments and didn't stop at the first one doesn't seem to bother them.

For good reason St. Paul called charity the greatest of all the gifts (1 Cor 13). For by this mutual love of Jesus' followers, the Church is known. And to all who meet us this charity should overflow.

Anthony never said that the love of our brothers in Christ would always be easy. He merely said that without it Christians will surely stray off course, neither following the Lord nor leading others to him.

The Church:
Our Only Salvation

"Sing this song in the Church of God. 'A strong city have we in Sion; for the Savior sets up walls and ramparts to protect us' (Is 26:1). Sion is Holy Church, the city of our strength, apart from which there is no salvation. In her has our Savior been placed as a wall

and a rampart, in his divinity and in his humanity.
And thus fortified by the wall of the Incarnate Word,
the Church will continue in peace and security until
the end."

Anthony again stresses the closeness of Christ and
his Church. Indeed, we are told that "apart from the
Church there is no salvation": a troubling statement.
What did Anthony mean by it? Presumably he
understood it as the Church today interprets it: a)
there is no salvation apart from Jesus Christ and b)
Jesus is presented to mankind only through his
followers, the Church. But it hasn't always been so
obvious to everyone what Catholics meant when they
used that statement. Indeed in the late 1940's a few
American Catholics claimed that only baptized
Catholics could be saved. Not so, said Rome. Persons
can be saved who are not formally members of the
Catholic Church. Vatican II repeated and expanded
this teaching in its *Constitution on the Church*.

"But why be Catholic then?" many people ask
today. The question deserves a thoughtful answer.
Catholicism has handed on the Gospel and the
teachings of Jesus more completely than the other
Churches. In our sacraments believers see the saving
action of God applied to their lives. In the Eucharist
Christ becomes truly present to strengthen and unify
his followers. The apostolic character and unity of the
Church is best shown in the succession of bishops
under the successor of St. Peter — the pope. Also, we
believe that Scripture's best interpretation is within
the Catholic tradition.

Over the last 15 years many words have been
written on the "crisis of faith" among Christians. But

does this crisis stem from uncertainty or disbelief about the Jesus described in the Gospels? For a few people, perhaps that is the case. But more often, hasn't the crisis been over whether or not there is any real connection between Jesus Christ and those who profess to be his followers, the Church? In fact, aren't we finding many people today who say they believe in Jesus but not the Church?

For Anthony of Padua, knowing Jesus and the salvation he brought was impossible apart from recognizing the Church which spreads this Good News. Can we then set Christ and his Church in basic opposition to each other?

Christ: The Solid Foundation

"Upon the one foundation which is Christ (1 Cor 3:11) has the Church been built. Since Jesus is the rock on which the House of God is built (Mt 7:24), we need not fear for it if the rains of diabolical persecution fall upon it or the floods of heresy threaten to inundate it, or the winds of the world's contempt blow and beat against it. It stands fast and does not fall, because a wise man has built it on firm rock."

These words of Anthony are simple, but they draw out an important assurance of Christ. The Church will endure not because her members have all been holy and not because her leaders have always been wise, but because the Church is built on Christ and is charged with spreading the Gospel.

Where would Christians have been without this

assurance? When the Roman persecutions broke out, wouldn't Christians have faded away? Was it mere human obstinacy that brought them to the catacombs? Why wasn't Christianity snuffed out by the barbarian invasions? Or why didn't medieval Christians throw in the towel when faced with weakness and corruption in the Church's leaders and common people?

Anthony of Padua and Francis of Assisi saw that the Church of their day needed a lot of rebuilding. But why did they bother?

They bothered — as men and women have before and since them — because they realized that the Church is intended by God to preach the Gospel, to celebrate God's saving deeds, and to be a sign of his love for men until Christ returns. Some days will be dark but never so dark as to wipe out Christ's work.

Christ's assurance should not, however, lull us into smugness. The Church is built on Christ not so that believers can be lazy about their witness to Christ but partly so that they will not be frenzied over their work and the Church's future.

If Christ were not the solid foundation of the Church, then his followers would face two ugly alternatives: 1) despair of the Church; or 2) constant fretting that somehow everything depended completely on them and that only they stand between the Church's fruitful witness to Jesus or its annihilation. Without the promise that Jesus is the solid rock of the Church and will always be with it, Christianity would have worried itself to death — or despaired — centuries ago.

In 30 A.D. the Church was solidly built on Jesus. Today he is still its foundation.

Christ Still Acts in His Church

"Christ the Good Shepherd feeds us daily by the teachings of the Gospel and the sacraments of the Church. The sheep who follow him are the faithful members of the Church who daily offer themselves as the altar of his Passion and in the sacrifice of a contrite heart as victims who are spotless, holy and pleasing to God."

Anthony's quote shows a great faith in the Church, for he never physically saw Christ preach the Good News or work a miracle. Indeed, Anthony's experience of the Gospel and its saving power followed Jesus by 12 centuries.

No, Anthony saw the *Church* teaching the Gospel and celebrating the sacraments. But he believed that Christ was at work there.

But the great temptation of Christians is to separate Christ and his Church by opposing them to each other. True enough, we should not divinize the Church so as to assume that in *every* instance it acts as God wants it to. That would deny the Church's human element, and humanity is capable of sin. But the sinfulness of the Church's members should not convince us that Christ has abandoned his Church. On the contrary, he set his followers among mankind to preach the Good News until the end of time.

Sometimes we think that the people who heard Jesus preach had a great advantage over those who came after him. Faith was easy for Jesus' contemporaries, we may say, but hard for us who only see his Church. The Gospels tell a different story: Most of those who saw Jesus did not accept him. And

St. John's Gospel ends with a blessing on those who will believe in Jesus without seeing him (20:29). Yes, Jesus can still be recognized in his Church.

But Anthony quickly points out the self-giving expected of Jesus' followers. He almost echoes Jesus' words, "It is not those who say to me 'Lord, Lord' who will enter the kingdom of heaven, but the person who does the will of my Father in heaven" (Mt 7:21). But how many of us shrink from that *daily* offering of ourselves to the Father's will? Rather, don't we like to pick the time and place and circumstance of any sacrifice stemming from the Gospel? In fact, we are tempted to pick and choose even when we read the Gospels. And who but the Church confronts us with the *whole* Gospel — including the parts we tend to gloss over — and shows us how to live it?

Christ still acts for us through his Church. But it takes faith to see this.

The Shepherds of the Church

"Blessed is that bishop or priest who can truthfully say: 'I am a good shepherd.' This he cannot do unless in reality he is like the Good Shepherd and possessed of many virtues: holiness of life, knowledge of Holy Scripture, eloquence of tongue, constancy in prayer, mercy for the poor and the afflicted, solid discipline toward those subject to him, and solicitous care for the people of God entrusted to him. Let him be like the Son of Man (Rv 1:13) in the midst of the Church, the people of God, by his poverty, humility and patience, spirit of contemplation of God and the things of God,

and compassion for his fellowman. And let his face
shine like the sun in its power (Rv 1:16): for through
his face, that is, his works, men shall come to know
the inward man of God. If a priest is all of this, then
truly he could say, 'I am a good shepherd.' "

Anthony certainly appreciated Christ's shepherd
imagery, for 13th century priests were often not well-
trained and were sometimes a scandal to the Church.
God's people needed to hear his word and see his
loving mercy in action.

Anthony's shepherds are powerful preachers,
men well-versed in Scripture, prayerful and patient.
Without these qualities their work is undercut. But
when he lists "solicitous care for the people of God
entrusted to him," perhaps Anthony is pointing out a
virtue supporting many of the others. After all,
Anthony later says, the priest should be in the Church
as one having "compassion on his fellowman." That
he drew all these virtues out of the shepherd imagery
is not surprising.

For when Christ said that he was the Good
Shepherd, what did he stress? "The good shepherd is
one who lays down his life for his sheep" (Jn 10:11).
Elsewhere Christ asks his listeners: Who with 100
sheep wouldn't leave the 99 and go searching for the
lost one and rejoice over finding it? So heaven
rejoices over the salvation of repentant sinners
(Lk 15:4-7). In both stories Christ emphasized the risk
a shepherd must take for his sheep.

Fine, so what?

God's people need compassionate and holy
shepherds as much today as ever before. So pray for
priests and bishops. And when you see them

searching after God's alienated sons and daughters, remember who told them to do it and encourage them. And if you know a young man who thinks the priesthood might be his vocation, encourage him, please, to investigate whether this is his calling.

Priests: The Church's Healers

"No one is closer to us than he who healed our wounds, for the Head is one with his members. Let us therefore love him as our Lord and God."

Anthony's expressions are surprisingly popular. Many current spiritual writers and preachers are increasingly talking about Christ "healing wounds." Indeed, several years ago Henri Nouwen, a Dutch priest living in the U.S., entitled his best-selling book on ministry, *Wounded Healer.*

Those who heal — whether diseases of the body or sickness of the spirit — must know personally what being wounded means. A doctor or nurse with absolutely no personal experience of sickness would be unable to communicate with patients. So, too, Christians who minister to the spiritual needs and hungers of mankind must know personally the sense of brokenness from sin and of restoration and wholeness coming from Christ.

In June of 1975 I was ordained to the priesthood. A year later several close friends of mine were also ordained priests. They and I are called by Christ and his Church to be "wounded healers." We are not priests because we have never sinned or will never

81

again need the healing forgiveness of Jesus. No, says the Letter to the Hebrews, "Every high priest has been taken out of mankind and is appointed to act for men in their relations with God, to offer gifts and sacrifices for sins; and so he can sympathize with those who are ignorant or uncertain because he too lives in the limitations of weakness. That is why he has to make sin offerings for himself as well as for the people" (5: 1-3). Priests are chosen with the expectation that having seen their own sinfulness and received the forgiveness of God, they in turn may go out to help others turn from sin and ask for God's healing mercy.

And there are wounds to be healed. Some are caused by the thoughtlessness or malice of others, but many people carry heavier self-inflicted wounds, such as those resulting from a refusal to forgive another. And sometimes the offense — intended or not — occurred years ago. These self-inflicted wounds heal only when the suffering person will accept God's forgiveness for himself and will extend it to others — and leave the final judgment to God.

In Christ our brokenness can be mended, for we are members of his Body. If priests follow the Church's direction to model their lives "after the mystery of the Lord's cross," then they may help us see this healing Christ.

The Value of Confession

"Too many people are satisfied to confess only once a year when perhaps it would be better if they confessed every day! Man is so prone to sin, and his memory is so fickle that at evening he can hardly remember what he did that very morning. Why do such unhappy people keep putting off confession for so long a time? Why wait even till tomorrow, for how do you know if tomorrow will dawn for you? You're alive today, and tomorrow you'll be no more. So live today as though you were to die this very day. Nothing is more certain than death, but nothing more uncertain than the hour of our death.''

These words of Anthony remind us that postponing confession is sometimes a great temptation for us. Why do we presume there will always be another chance to receive today's graces? Why are we reluctant to accept absolution as a sign of God's forgiveness and of our rededication to his way?

Basically we are very often slow to admit our own sins and even slower to confess them to a priest who is Christ's minister, but also a fellow sinful human being. Often we may be tempted to "confess our sins to God directly" without the sacrament of Penance or the aid which the Church offers. God, however, invites us to receive his forgiveness and encouragement in an unmistakable way through his priests.

When the Prodigal Son finally admitted sinning against his father and against God, he hurried home for a reconciliation. The father was watching for his lost son and ran out to welcome him back. Indeed, the father cried, "This son of mine was dead, but now he is alive; he was lost, but now he has been found" (Lk 15:24). The Prodigal Son had not realized the greatness of his father's love. Asking only to be

considered a servant and not a son, he was
overwhelmed by his father's forgiveness.

We too do not know our heavenly Father, and so
we often fear a cold and harsh reception from him.
God, however, is always more ready to forgive us than
we are willing to admit our need of forgiveness. And
so God scans the homeward road for many more
repentant sinners than those he sees. And yet he
keeps waiting.

There is always time for confession, right? No,
says Anthony. "Live today as though you were to die
this very day." Morbid? Not really, for there is an
inherent urgency about love. True love is always
impatient until it can be shown and expressed.
Whatever obstacles block the way must be removed
now, not sometime in the indefinite future. It only
makes sense to be ready when our loving Father calls.

Penance: A Second Baptism

"The sacrament of Penance is itself a kind of
baptism of water and the Holy Spirit, of the spirit of
sorrow and contrition and of the water of a tearful
confession. Thereby, whoever has lost by mortal sin
the innocence and grace his first Baptism gave him
can recover such treasures by the power of this
second baptism."

Anthony had a special concern that his listeners
celebrate the sacrament of Penance. He knew that the
damage caused by sins can be healed by contrition
and a humble telling of one's sins.

When Pope Paul first announced the 1975 Holy Year, he said: "We need above all to reestablish a genuine, vital and happy relationship with God, to be reconciled with him in humility and love, so that from this first basic harmony the whole world of our experience may express a need and acquire a virtue of reconciliation in charity and justice with men, to whom we immediately give the new title of 'brothers.' " Therefore, Pope Paul hoped that the Holy Year might bring a "revaluation of repentance as the essential element of the Christian spirit and a fresh awareness of the sacrament of Penance as a means of nourishing this spirit."

Anthony would have appreciated this concern that Catholics rediscover the value of this sacrament and that they see their reconciliation with God as the basis for healing their other fractured relationships: within themselves, with others and with creation itself. It is now becoming increasingly common for Catholics to refer to Penance as the sacrament of reconciliation. For here believers can express their sorrow for sin and receive the assurance that God is always ready to forgive the contrite and again to help them in living out their baptismal promises. And also very important, here believers can see that the Church also forgives them, welcomes them and encourages their good resolution.

Sin is never strictly private in its effects because human beings are relational. God made them that way. Thus, the forgiveness of sin also shows that the Church welcomes back the contrite sinner.

The New Rite of Penance, I

"Holy Job, whose name can be interpreted to mean the 'sorrowful man,' contemplating his miseries, cried out: 'I will not spare my utterance; I will speak in the anguish of my spirit, I will complain in the bitterness of my soul' (Jb 7:11).

"Here we have a brief and most useful example of a good confession. He does not 'spare his utterance' who plainly and openly confesses his sin and its circumstances. He speaks 'in anguish of spirit' who in confession accuses himself with contrite heart and troubled spirit and seeks not to excuse himself but to judge himself for his wrongdoings. He complains (or talks) 'in the bitterness of his soul' who holds nothing back, hides nothing, but seeks rather to renew and deepen his sorrow. Subjecting himself wholly to the judgment of the priest, he says with Saul: 'Lord, what wilt thou have me do?' Full of distrust of self and of complete confidence in the advice of the confessor, he says with Samuel: 'Speak, Lord, for your servant is listening.'

"Thus you have a picture of what the penitent must see (his sins and sinfulness), what he must speak (in a contrite confession of guilt), and what he must hear (the voice of God through the ministry of the priest)."

In sermons like the one above, Anthony of Padua emphasized his listeners' need to go to confession.

During 1976 a new rite for celebrating the sacrament of Penance was introduced in the U.S. Late in 1973, Pope Paul approved the new rite for the universal Church; the U.S. bishops decided to introduce it here in 1976.

Why another change? Vatican II had directed that all the sacraments should be revised to stress especially their close connection with the Word of God and with the activity of the whole Church.

What was changed? There is an option to confess face-to-face. After greeting the penitent with an invitation to prayer, the confessor will read a selection from a Scripture passage "which proclaims God's mercy and calls men to conversion." After the sins have been confessed, the priest gives a suitable penance and then both pray for the mercy of God. The absolution formula now stresses God's initiative in reconciling and the Church's reconciling ministry.

This quote emphasizes the penitent's need to see sin clearly, to acknowledge it and receive God's forgiveness. I feel sure that Anthony would see this new rite as the Church's sincere effort to help her children reconcile themselves first with their Father and then with each other.

The New Rite of Penance, II

"Those who are truly sorry for their sins do not seek excuses to make their sins seem less than they are. Instead, conscious of their guilt and shame before the eyes of God rather than of men, they clearly and bluntly reveal (to the confessor) the wickedness they have done. But there are others who lose their tongues in the confessional and babble their sins in a whisper. They weren't ashamed to commit them, but they are ashamed to confess them."

Anthony's words show his experience and sensitivity as a confessor. Since some people are more conscious of their guilt before God than of their shame before men, they confess straightforwardly. Others mumble their sins.

The new rite of Penance stresses how eager God is for the sinner's restoration to health. God is always more ready to forgive sincere sorrow than sinners are ready to ask forgiveness. Those who confess straightforwardly have long known this. But those who "lose their tongues in the confessional" have likely been less conscious of God's great desire to forgive them and have been more worried about what the confessor might think of them or say to them.

But why is the confessor there in the first place? He represents the God who desires our wholeness and the Church which seeks to aid that reconciliation with God and with other believers. In the new rite the priest immediately invites the penitent to trust in the mercy of God. Once the sins have been confessed and pardon has been asked, the priest prays the new absolution formula: "God, the Father of mercies, through the death and resurrection of his Son has reconciled the world to himself and sent the Holy Spirit among us for the forgiveness of sins; through the ministry of the Church may God give you pardon and peace, and I absolve you from your sins in the name of the Father, and of the Son, and of the Holy Spirit." Then with a praise of God's mercy, the priest dismisses the penitent.

The new rite allows face-to-face confession. Some who use this option will be self-conscious at first and may wonder, "What will the priest think of me for this?" The priest is there to be an obvious sign of the mercy of God and the Church's care for sinners. Understanding sin and suggesting appropriate remedies is part of his ministry. Also, the priest's obligation to the seal of confession has not changed, and he himself still needs to seek the forgiveness of God and the assistance of the Church.

Now is the perfect time to celebrate the new rite of Penance.

The Eucharist and Human Hungers

"Nothing apart from God can satisfy the human heart which is truly in search of him."

Anthony of Padua never participated in a Eucharistic Congress, for they date back only to 1881. But Anthony had a great devotion to Christ's presence in the Blessed Sacrament. This quote matches the theme of the International Eucharistic Congress which met in Philadelphia in August of 1976.

That theme was "The Eucharist and the Hungers of the Human Family." In the 1975 pastoral statement by that same title, the U.S. bishops said: "In the Eucharist, which is Jesus really present, God satisfies our deepest hungers. The Sacrifice of the Mass is Christ's supreme act of reconciliation." Later they said that the Eucharist "responds to our needs and concerns — our many hungers — as human beings." Each day of the Congress celebrated the Eucharist's relationship to a different human hunger: for God, bread, freedom and justice, the Spirit, truth, understanding, peace, and Jesus, the Bread of Life.

Anthony shared these eight hungers. He longed to know and serve God, to promote fair treatment for the poor of his day, to spread the Good News and to establish peace among warring factions in Italian city-states. Surely he saw the Eucharist as nourishment for all these hungers and as an incentive to satisfy them.

When Anthony says that only God can satisfy the human heart which is truly in search of him, he re-echoes Augustine of Hippo's famous statement: "You have made us for yourself, O God, and our hearts are restless until they rest in you" (Confessions 1,1). Like Augustine, Anthony tried to satisfy his deepest hungers apart from God, but both men eventually brought those yearnings before their Creator.

Have you ever tried to satisfy the hungers of your heart apart from God? Have you envied someone's good fortune and wished it away from that person and onto yourself? Have you ever treated someone else as a thing and not as a child of God? Can you recall ever stealing someone's goods or even his good name? If you have ever sinned, you have attempted to fulfill a basic human hunger selfishly apart from God.

We have perhaps temporarily accepted substitutes for God: money, power, sex, prestige. No one of these things is evil in itself, but any of them can become *distorted* and made the independent goal of one's life. And yet in themselves they can never completely satisfy us, for they point us back to our Creator.

In heaven all our hungers will be satisfied; meanwhile, the Eucharist is a pledge of that future glory and a guard against discouragement as we carry on Christ's work.

Eucharist: A Way of Life

"During the meal, Jesus took bread, blessed it and broke it as a sign that not without his free consent was his body to be broken in death. The humanity of Christ is like the grape because it was crushed in the wine press of the cross so that his blood flowed forth over all the earth. This blood the Lord gave to the apostles to drink. 'This is my blood of the new covenant, which shall be shed for many unto the forgiveness of sins.' How great is the charity of the beloved! How great the love of the bridegroom for his spouse, the Church! His own blood, which in the future he was to pour forth for her in the hands of the faithful, he offered to her today with his most holy hands."

Following the Gospel of John, Anthony says that life was not seized from Christ. He laid it down freely for the salvation of all men and women — but only after he had given us the Eucharist.

Awesome as Christ's gift of the Eucharsit is, we can allow ourselves to become quite used to it. Even though we join in the Mass regularly, we can blunt its meaning, its power to reorder our lives. We can assume that doing the Father's will was no sacrifice for Jesus. Gradually we may fail to appreciate the price of our salvation.

The Eucharist is the greatest present-day sign of Christ's love for his Church. How often do we let it become a sign of disunity? Some people strenuously object to the greeting of peace before Communion. Others can become quite nasty about the kind of music they prefer at Mass. Some people carefully avoid receiving Communion from lay distributors! A few believers introduce innovations which make the Eucharist almost unrecognizable as Christ's self-offering and as the prayer of the Church.

Christ meant the Eucharist as a sign of unity, of his continuing presence among and for believers, but we can turn this gift into a battleground.

St. Paul had to scold the Christians in Corinth for bringing their factions into the Eucharist. Every time you eat this bread and drink this cup, said Paul (1 Cor 11:26), you proclaim the Lord's death until he comes. If we fail to recognize the body of the Lord in the transformed bread and wine, we celebrate the Eucharist unworthily. Forming factions around our personal preference can also mean not recognizing the body of the Lord in his assembled community!

For Catholics the Eucharist is a way of life. If we want to share in Christ's saving death and resurrection, we will find a way to maintain the unity and charity which the Eucharist represents.

Praying With Our Heart

"We can pray in a threefold way: with our heart, with our mouth, with our hands. Of the first the wise man says: 'The prayer of the humble pierces the clouds' (Sir 35:21) and reaches the home of God. Of the second the psalmist cries: 'May my prayer come unto You' (Ps 87:2). Of the third the Apostle exhorts us: 'Pray constantly' (1 Thes 5:17), in the sense that he does not cease to pray who does not cease to do good."

If this quote from Anthony were any longer, he probably would have stressed the crucial importance of the first way, prayer with our heart. For it is obvious that sincere prayer with our lips and genuine prayer with our hands are rooted in interior prayer.

Otherwise, the melody and the lyrics clash, so to speak. If verbal prayer and works of charity proceed from some motive other than interior prayer, to that extent they are not genuine prayer. But oral prayer and works of charity flowing from a devout heart are strong indeed.

Consider the story of the Pharisee and the tax collector in the Temple (Lk 18:9-14). The Pharisee's prayer cited two works of charity: fasting twice a week and paying tithes beyond what the Law of Moses required. Yet the Pharisee congratulated himself that he was so much better than other people — specifically, the tax collector behind him. And how did the tax collector pray? He asked forgiveness. He truly prayed, says Christ, and so went home "at rights with God." Christ does not say fasting and paying tithes are evil and worthless — simply that they are not genuine prayer unless they come from a prayerful heart.

For sometimes it will be easier to say many prayers or perform works of charity than to pray to God from the heart. At other times we will be unable to recollect ourselves for anything more than these verbal and manual prayers. But if these prayers thrive and interior prayer wanes, then we have truly built on sand instead of solid rock (Lk 6:47-49). And we will have fallen into the empty formalism condemned by God so strongly in the prophets (e.g., Is 1:10-17, Mi 6:6-8).

But we may have difficulties with interior prayer. Assuming we create time for it, next we are likely to ask: What does it do? What does it produce? Why take the time? It is in the prayers of the heart especially that our deepening conversion to God occurs. But whether or not such conversion is immediately evident, interior prayer is primarily for the praise of God.

There are, says Anthony, three ways of praying. But if the prayer of the heart is not the basis of the other two, they are indeed planted in strange soil.

Making Time and Place

"Alas, how many disturbing thoughts go through our heart. As a result we lack the leisure to enjoy the bread of heavenly delights and to taste the joys of interior contemplation. For that reason the good Master invites us: 'Come apart from the restless throng into a desert place, into solitude of mind and body.' When a man withdraws from the turbulence of the world and rests in quiet and solitude, tasting the bread of tears as he thinks over his sins, then does the Lord make himself known to him."

Distraction is not the invention of the 20th century, as these words of Anthony show. His listeners knew well the hazards to a recollected life.

Such as? Anthony identifies a lack of leisure as the first obstacle. Yes, but don't we in the 20th century have a lot of leisure time — more than people had in Anthony's day? Generally we spend less time working than they did, but that doesn't necessarily mean more leisure, which also includes creativity and a slower pace. Too often we have so many things to do that there is no time for the interior life.

The second obstacle is the lack of a "desert," a place in which "to come apart from the restless throng." How easily can you find rest and solitude?

A third obstacle dwarfs the first two: Do we really feel a *need* for the desert, for a time and a place to examine our life before God? If we firmly answer "yes," then the time and place are easier to find. Perhaps that weekend retreat advertised in the Sunday bulletin wouldn't be such a bad idea. Maybe a little extra time in the morning for meditation would be good.

Yes, but some people suspect this time apart is really an escape. It is all well and good to contemplate in the desert, but what about one's responsibilities back in the city? Can prayer solve the problems of educating the young or feeding the hungry? Not exactly, but then is it really to give more time to these responsibilities that Christians shun prayer in solitude? Christians such as Pope John XXIII have found time for both prayer and action.

People will eventually give themselves time for rest, for regaining the equilibrium in their lives. But for Christ's followers part of that balance ought to include a joyful praise of God's wonders, a sober reflection on personal sins and then some thought on how to follow Christ more faithfully. After all, in prayer and solitude the Lord makes himself known to us. How can we wait for him somewhere else?

Waiting for the Lord

"Patience is one of the fruits of the Holy Spirit in us. Practically, we are required to be patient in many ways: for there are some things, trials and crosses, which come to us from God; others, temptations and enticements, that come to us from our old adversary the devil; still other difficulties that arise from our neighbor: persecution, complaints, unjust accusations. Against all these we must be ever on our guard lest we give way to complaining against the trials our Maker sends us; lest again we be led astray into sin, which is what the devil wants; or to be overly distrubed by the thoughtlessness or unkindness of others. For if we want to have our own way always, aren't we really seeking our reward here below in the things of this life? Let us couple patience and long-suffering in the spirit of meekness and faith (and so bring forth fruit in patience)!"

Anthony's examples show he knew that patience is never easy. Advent has traditionally been a time to remember the Jewish people's long, patient wait for the Messiah. Like them we must wait and practice patience, but how shall we do it? What is its cost?

Without hope, waiting makes no sense. Yet we know hope is often difficult to maintain. Other people fail us and we fail them; we fail ourselves. The temptation of despairing of God's and others' love for us is always a possibility. Nevertheless, hope says that God's love for us is constant and that he will never test us or allow us to be tested beyond our strength as aided by his grace. Maintaining hope is waiting's first cost.

Advent remembers the many thousand years of expectation between Adam's fall and Christ's birth. But God's Chosen People suffered through many dark times during those years. And that is the second cost of waiting. Perhaps you've never thought of suffering this way, but did you ever wait for something important to happen to you without suffering?

What then shall we do for Advent this year? How shall we prepare for Christ's coming? If we reflect and pray over hope as crucial to waiting, then maybe we can bring some hope to a person on the verge of despair. And if we believe that every waiting has its suffering, then perhaps we can help someone bear a cross arising from waiting — for example, anxiety over recovery from an illness. While Advent is a time for special prayer, it is also a time for humble deeds flowing out of prayer. Where? Look around and choose.

We are not alone in being patient. God's patience and his faithful love for man are our guide. And if in the time before Christmas we grow closer to God's patience and appreciate its cost, then we will know better the tremendous and costly gift that Jesus is.

Mary's Example: "Fertile Land"

"From Christ, as from the center, stream forth all graces to us who are in the circumference. When the soul lies before him like fertile land, it is a Garden of Eden in which bloom the rose of love, the violet of humility, and the lily of purity."

Anthony's words above are a good start for a Christmas meditation, for they remind us that all good gifts are from God and that of God's many gifts to us Jesus is the greatest.

Because Mary's soul was before Christ "like fertile land," she cooperated with God's plan and answered the angel, "Let it be done to me as you say." Joseph likewise cooperated in God's plan as a support to Mary and a model for Jesus. A soul ready for Christ is truly like the Garden of Eden in which creation is alive and fresh.

Jesus was born in poor circumstances. But Mary and Joseph were rich in grace, and virtue bloomed in them. God could have come on this earth without their help. Similarly, God could reveal himself to us without the aid of any person. But he prefers our cooperation.

Renewal and reconciliation, two constant needs in Christian life, do not occur all by themselves. As Anthony said, from Christ stream all graces to us. But those graces are not forced on us. We in the circumference can send those graces back or spread them further, widening the circle of people who acknowledge Jesus as Lord.

Individually and as a Church we will need the renewal which greater fidelity to Christ brings. Our purity of heart must become deeper, and the need for reconciliation on all levels continues.

How shall we further renewal and reconciliation? Most basically we can follow the example of Mary and Joseph by offering ourselves to God "as fertile land." From Christ come all graces, but they still need a place to grow. "Bloom where you are planted" says the banner.

A King of Lowly Birth

"Jesus Christ is the King of kings, who has done battle to deliver us from the hands of our enemies. He came forth from the bosom of the Father, and humbled himself by coming into the womb of the Blessed Virgin Mary and taking to himself the flesh of our humanity. His food was to do the will of him who sent him and accomplish his work.

"Behold, then, your king! Jeremiah says of him: 'There is none like you, O Lord: great are you, great and mighty is your name. Who would not fear you, king of the nations?' This is indeed he of whom St. John cries: 'He has as his garment and on his thigh a name written: King of kings and Lord of lords' (Rv 19:16). His 'garment' is the swaddling clothes, his 'thigh' the flesh he took. For in Nazareth he was crowned with our flesh as with a diadem; in Bethlehem he is wrapped as though in royal purple. Because these were the first insignia of his ruling power, his opponents tried to rob him of both, stripping him of his clothes in his passion and nailing his flesh to the cross. And yet this only brought his kingdom to perfection. He had crown and purple but lacked the scepter — and this he received as he took up his cross and went forth to the place called Calvary. He was crowned with honor and glory because he suffered death (Heb 2:9). Behold then how your king has come to you, in meekness and suffering, desirous of being loved and served and not feared because of his power."

Anthony's devotion to the Christ Child, as expressed above, recalls Francis of Assisi who years

before popularized the Christmas crib and
encouraged Christians to meditate on the manner of
the Lord's birth.

Why did the King of kings come into this world
defenseless — like the rest of us at birth? Anthony
and Francis answer, "To show us how strong is the
power of God and how much his ways are different
from ours."

Truthfully, couldn't we have planned better
circumstances for Jesus' birth? And aren't we a little
embarrassed by the way God chose?

God acts in strange ways — from our viewpoint.
Instead of a Savior born to Jewish royalty, God sent
his Son to a working-class family, and so we cannot
attribute Jesus' "success" to advantages of birth. God
often shows his power through apparent weakness —
even through us.

This year, what shall we learn about God and his
ways from meditating on the Christmas crib?

Mary: Guide to Christmas Faith

"We pray you, our Lady, loving Mother of God, on
this feast of the birthday of your Son, whom you bore
as virgin and wrapped in swaddling clothes and
placed in a manger, beg forgiveness of him for us, and
by your mercy heal the burns which the fire of our
sins has inflicted on us. Thus healed may we merit to
share the feast of eternal joys through the
graciousness of your Son who this day was born of
you, O glorious virgin. To him be honor and glory
forever."

As these words express, Anthony had a special reverence for the birthday of Christ, the day on which God's only Son and instrument of our salvation took flesh for all the world to see. And so Anthony honored Mary also, for she cooperated with God's mysterious plan in a special way.

Mary and Joseph provided the natural family setting in which Jesus could grow "in wisdom and age and grace before God and man" (Lk 2:52). God chose that his Son be raised from infancy to manhood in a family.

Mary can be a model for our own observance of Christmas, for her faith was strong that God would fulfill what he had promised. A cave and a manger were not a very promising beginning for the Son of God, but Mary's faith was not weakened. Shepherds called from the fields were not the most likely well-wishers for the King of Kings and Prince of Peace. If ever there was a test of faith, Christ's birth at Bethlehem was it.

We tend to think that Mary had all the advantages where faith is concerned. True, she did not suffer the effects of original sin, yet this did not provide her with a roadmap to her future or that of Jesus. She too had to suffer and to keep pondering many things in her heart (Lk 2:51). Actually, because we know Mary from the Gospels and from tradition, we have at least the advantage of positive proof that Mary's faith was sustained and amply rewarded. On that night of Christ's birth, Mary relied only on God's strength to accomplish his plan.

As we celebrate this year the birth of Jesus, we ask Mary to be our guide in faith and to strengthen us when we are tempted to waver or to doubt God's love and care for us. God is indeed good to his people. Of this great truth, Mary's faith at Bethlehem can be a constant reminder.

Mary: Sign of God's New Covenant

"Our Mediatrix, the most holy Virgin Mary, has brought about peace between God and the sinners. As the rainbow in the clouds (Gn 9:13) after the Flood was the sign of the covenant between God and the earth, so Mary is truly the sign of the covenant and peace between God and the sinner."

Anthony's words reveal an abiding devotion to the Blessed Virgin Mary. In this he follows Francis of Assisi, who placed his Gospel brotherhood under her patronage. For her faithful cooperation in God's plan, for her poor and simple life and for her great charity, Francis and Anthony had a great respect.

What then does Anthony mean in calling our Blessed Mother "the sign of the covenant and peace between God and the sinner"? He suggests that just as a rainbow in the sky was God's pledge to Noah not to destroy the earth by water, so Mary signifies the new covenant between God and mankind. But she is not a sign of what God will not do (destroy the earth by water) but of what God has always intended and has now done (sent his only Son for the salvation of all men and women).

Mary is this sign because of her great faith and willingness to cooperate with God's plan. At her Annunciation she did not foresee the future in detail but rather said, "Be it done to me as you say." When Jesus was born and when he was lost in the Temple, she could not predict how he would grow up and exactly what he would do, but on both occasions "she treasured all these things and pondered them in her heart" (Lk 2:19, 51).

The United States bishops in their 1973 pastoral *Behold Your Mother* said: "The Gospels provide few details of Mary's life; but they do delineate a remarkable portrait of the woman who gave herself whole-heartedly to her Son and his mission in perfect faith, love and obedience. What Mary began on earth in association with the saving mission of Jesus, she continues still, in union with the risen Christ" *(69)*.

Faith led Mary to consent to becoming the mother of Jesus, and her faith has thus made her mother of us all. Perhaps today we can ask God to help us grow in faith as Mary did. And maybe we can let that faith overflow in a work of charity such as Mary performed. Do you have a lonely friend you have been meaning to visit? Can you make a contribution toward feeding the hungry?

Mary is unquestionably a sign of the new covenant. But are we ready to read and follow that sign?

A Christmas Prayer

"We beseech you, O heavenly Father, through our Lord Jesus Christ, whom you have made 'the sacrifice that takes our sins away' (1 Jn 4:10), to receive through him our offerings and prayers, and through him give us the grace to be reconciled to you and to our brothers here on earth and, being thus at peace with you and with them, to offer our sacrifices of praise with the holy angels before your golden altar in the Jerusalem which is above. This we ask of you who, three in one, are blessed forever!"

In this short prayer Anthony describes the entire mission of Christ: to be a sacrifice for our sins and to enable us to be reconciled with the Father and with our brothers and sisters. Only then may we return worthy praise to God.

Kenosis is the Greek word for self-emptying, for laying aside what a person has. The early Church praised Jesus for his kenosis, for becoming a humble servant obedient even to death on the cross (Phil 2:6-11).

Christmas celebrates Jesus' kenosis and the obedience and self-emptying of Mary and Joseph. Jesus was born of a humble virgin whose faith allowed her to brave the unknown. He was born as the foster-son of a man who trusted God and cooperated in a plan the outcome of which he could not foresee.

Following Jesus involves us in kenosis, the basis for all reconciliation — literally, rejoining a broken circle. Reconciliation always follows a stand-off and requires one side to make an extra effort to heal the existing wound. There is no reconciliation without kenosis.

Jesus' life and death allows us to be reconciled to God, to be made whole before our Creator and in relation to all God's sons and daughters. Adam's sin shattered the harmony of creation and wounded humanity's trust for God. That sin also introduced disunity between Adam and Eve and among their descendants. Jesus confronts the fragmentation of sin with the unifying effect of salvation.

Christmas often comes and goes so quickly we hardly take time to reflect on the great mystery and the consequent attitude of thanksgiving we should have toward the Father for this most awesome gift of his Son. Our faith indeed recognizes that Jesus' offering himself to the Father in the Christmas Mass is already our supreme thanks to the Father. And we continue this prayer of gratitude as we kneel at the crib or pause to say grace at our Christmas meal.

But such prayers of thanksgiving should find special expression in a life imitating the self-sacrifice of Jesus. This Christmas could we make an *extra* effort to bridge a division between us and someone else? Can we match our admiration of Christmas music and rituals with generous self-sacrifice?

For those who, after the example of Jesus, respond to the Father's love by an emptying of self, Christmas will be special indeed!

Mary: Our Mother in Faith

" 'A thing of wonder, says the wise man (Sir 42:2), is the sun, the work of the Most High.' The Virgin Mary is an even greater work of wonder, for she was the bridal chamber wherein the Son of God took flesh, the sanctuary of the Spirit, the dwelling of the most Blessed Trinity, for 'He who created me rested in my tent' (Sir 24:8). O work indeed of wonder, for the Son

of God made her more beautiful than all other
creatures and holier than all the saints, and then in
her took on human form and became one of us."

All devotion to Mary ultimately traces itself back
to that faith-filled moment in Nazareth when she said
"yes" to God's request. Anthony's quote indicates our
need always to remember Mary's faith as we consider
her privilege of being Christ's mother.

Anthony refers to Mary as "the sanctuary of the
Spirit, the dwelling of the most Blessed Trinity." She
is a powerful reminder of God's continuing presence
to mankind. Thus, Catholicism has long honored her
under the title "Ark of the Covenant," for like the Old
Testament Ark of the Covenant, she reminds God's
people of his unfailing plan — now accomplished in
Jesus Christ.

Jesus, born of Mary without the aid of a human
father, is the sign of a new creation, of the fullness of
God's plan for union with him. But Mary's claim to
holiness is not based simply on her one-time
cooperation in Jesus' conception. No, throughout her
life Mary opened herself to the word of God and acted
on it — even to the point of suffering.

St. Luke particularly stressed Mary's faith in two
somewhat odd stories. Jesus once was told that his
relatives were outside waiting to see him, and he
replied, "My mother and my brothers are those who
hear the word of God and put it into practice" (Lk 8:
21). Another time, a woman praised the womb that
bore Jesus and the breasts that nursed him, but he
answered, "Still happier those who hear the word of
God and keep it" (Lk 11:28). Seemingly, these

incidents divert attention away from Mary, but through them Jesus is actually offering Mary as the perfect example of hearing the word of God and acting on it.

The Church has not forgotten Mary's faith. At every Mass, that faith is recalled in the Eucharistic Prayer. Catholics worldwide are still reciting the rosary and meditating on Mary's cooperation.

Mary is called our mother in faith not only because she was the mother of Jesus but also because her entire life exemplified an unshakable trust in the faithfulness of God. Indeed, not even the cross of Jesus could overwhelm her faith.

Mary kept herself alert to the Word of God; she can help us do the same.

Each year on June 13 thousands come to Padua to honor St. Anthony.

Part III: St. Anthony
Devotions and Prayers

1231
1195
_____
36 yrs. old,
when died

Devotions to St. Anthony

Anthony died in 1231, and immediately people came to pray at his tomb and ask his intercession. After he was canonized the next year, devotion to Anthony spread worldwide through the help of the Franciscans, the Italians, and the Portuguese.

Nine Tuesdays. Perhaps the devotion most closely associated with Anthony is the nine Tuesdays. The devotion originated in 1617 when a childless wife prayed to Anthony that she and her husband might have a child. Anthony is said to have appeared to her and told her to pray before his statue in the local Franciscan church on nine consecutive Tuesdays and her prayer would be answered. The child was born and the devotion spread.

Some time later a practice of visiting any church on 13 Tuesdays arose. Anthony died on June 13, and he was buried on a Tuesday.

There are no indulgences specifically connected with either the nine Tuesdays or the 13 Tuesdays. The 1968 *Enchiridion of Indulgences,* however, lists partial indulgences for reading Scripture and visiting the Blessed Sacrament and plenary indulgences for reciting the rosary in Church and making the Way of the Cross. Any or all of these might be part of Tuesday devotions to St. Anthony.

St. Anthony Lilies. The practice of blessing lilies on St. Anthony's feast day comes from the 18th century. After the French Revolution, the Franciscans were expelled from the Mediterranean island of Corsica. The Franciscan church there was abandoned, but the people continued to use it for their annual St. Anthony celebration on June 13. Some months after one of these celebrations a man wandered into the church and found the lilies from the celebration still fresh.

The lily, of course, is a traditional Christian symbol for purity, and the custom arose of blessing lilies on Anthony's feast. Leo XIII gave the custom his approval, and the Franciscans have a special blessing for this occasion. When the lilies are taken home and dried, they are intended to remind people of the need to pray in times of temptation.

St. Anthony Bread. The oldest of the St. Anthony devotions arose sometime before 1263 when a young child drowned near St. Anthony's basilica, then under construction. His mother sought the aid of St.

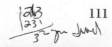

Anthony and promised that if the child were restored to life, she would give to the poor a measure of corn equal to the boy's weight. Little Tomasino was restored to life.

In some places the custom arose of placing children under the protection of St. Anthony. Some parents would donate grain equal to the child's weight for the poor patients in the city hospital. More wealthy parents might donate silver which would be used to purchase bread for the poor.

In the late 19th century the custom of donating money for the poor in honor of St. Anthony began, and from the church of St. Anthony in Rome, bread is now daily distributed to the poor. Other charitable works (including educating young men for the priesthood and aiding foreign missions) have benefitted from this custom. The Pious Union of St. Anthony, headquartered at St. Anthony's in Rome, asks its members to give a donation to the poor whenever they receive a favor through the intercession of St. Anthony. St. Anthony's "bread" continues under a new form.

Chaplet of St. Anthony. During the 19th century some people in Padua began to recite 13 Our Fathers, Hail Marys and Glories in thanksgiving for favors granted after having prayed the Responsory of St. Anthony. This is known as the Rosary or Chaplet of St. Anthony. It is composed of 13 groups of three beads each. On the first bead of each three is said the Our Father, on the second, the Hail Mary, and on the third, Glory be, etc.

Finder of Lost Objects. Soon after Anthony died,

The stone of the tomb of St. Anthony in Padua has been worn smooth by the touch of millions of pilgrims.

people began praying to him for the return of lost and stolen things. Why St. Anthony? The story says that when Anthony was in France, a novice, grown weary of religious life, had carried off Anthony's book of psalms which contained notes for Anthony's lectures to the friar-students. Anthony prayed for God's mercy on the thief and the return of the book. The novice did return the book, a rare and valuable item in those days, and was re-admitted to the community. Soon Anthony's help was sought in finding other lost or stolen items.

St. Anthony Prayers

Prayer to St. Anthony

Doctor of the Gospel, light of holy Church, lover of souls, true son of Francis of Assisi, Anthony of Padua! Help us have a true and solid devotion to you, and imitate your life and work for God and souls. Hold before us the Book of books, Holy Scripture, the source of your wisdom. Be to us a teacher of the ways of God and the gospel of our Lord Jesus Christ.

Put into our hearts the *flame* of love, the fire of divine charity, that we may love our merciful Father in heaven; that the King of kings, as you said, may reign in our hearts and purify them of all evil; that we may love our neighbor, that is, every man, as you taught.

May the *lily* of your chastity, your spirit of prayer, make us faithful to the vows of our Baptism, to the vows of marriage or of religious life. But to our day also an apostle and teacher, that we may live with you the gospel of Christ and grow with you in him.

Holy Teacher of the Gospel, pray that the spirit of the gospel may reach all men of all nations, beginning with ourselves. Pray that the spirit of Christian love and unity may fill the people of God, and bring all his children together again as one flock with one Shepherd. Amen.

A Prayer of Thanksgiving

O glorious wonder-worker, St. Anthony, father of the poor and comforter of the troubled, you have come to my assistance with great kindness, and strengthened me abundantly. I come to you to give you my heartfelt thanks. Accept my offering and with it my serious promise, which I now renew, to live always in the love of Jesus and of my neighbor. Continue to shield me graciously by your protection, and obtain for me the final grace of being able one day to enter the kingdom of heaven, to sing with you the everlasting mercies of God. Amen.

The Responsory of St. Anthony

If then you ask for miracles:
Death, error, all calamities,
The leprosy and demons fly
And health succeeds infirmities.

The sea obeys and fetters break,
And lifeless limbs thou dost restore;
While treasures lost are found again
When young or old thine aid implore.

All dangers vanish at thy prayer,
And every need doth quickly flee:
Let those who know thy power tell,
Let Paduans say, "These are of thee."

To Father, Son, may glory be,
And Holy Spirit enternally.
The sea obeys . . .

V. Pray for us, Blessed Anthony.
R. That we may be made worthy of the promises of Christ.

Let us pray:

O God, may the votive commemoration of Blessed Anthony, your confessor and doctor, be a source of joy to your Church, that she may always be fortified with spiritual assistance, and may deserve to possess eternal joy. Through Christ, our Lord. Amen.

Prayer for Lost Objects

Saint Anthony, it seems that God has chosen you to remind us that he's not too busy to be concerned about the little problems of our life—when we lose our contact lenses, our wallets, our homework or our keys. Help me to keep my calm and my common sense as I look for what I have lost. Help me to be a little better organized, a little more careful in the future.

And while you're working on this loss, please help me also not to lose what is much more important: my gift of faith in a loving Father; my confidence in his endless mercy; my love for him in my brothers and sisters. Amen.

Prayer for the Blessing of St. Anthony Lilies

O God, the creator and preserver of the human race, lover of spotless purity, giver of spiritual grace and bestower of eternal salvation: by Thy holy blessing bless these lilies which we Thy suppliants present to Thee this day as a token of gratitude in honor of Thy confessor Saint Anthony, and which we beg to be plessed.

By the saving sign of Thy most holy cross, shed on them a heavenly dew. O most clement Lord, who hast given them to man for the sweetness of their fragrance and the healing of infirmities, fill and strengthen them with such power, that in whatever sickness they may be used, or in whatever house or place they be put, or wherever borne with devotion, through the intercession of this Thy same servant Anthony, they may put to flight the evil spirits, lead to holy continence, keep away all ailments, and bring peace and grace to all who serve Thee. Through Christ our Lord. Amen.*

*Devotion to St. Anthony of Padua for Private or Public Use, Franciscan Herald Press, 1954, p. 47.

Litany of St. Anthony

(For Private Devotion)

Lord, have mercy on us! *Christ, have mercy on us!*
Lord, have mercy on us!
Christ, hear us! *Christ, graciously hear us!*
God, the Father of Heaven, *have mercy on us!*
God, the Son, Redeemer of the world, *have mercy on us!*
God, the Holy Spirit, *have mercy on us!*
Holy Trinity, one God, *have mercy on us!*
Holy Mary,
Holy Father Francis,
St. Anthony of Padua,
St. Anthony, Glory of the Order of Friars Minor,
St. Anthony, Martyr in desiring to die for Christ,
St. Anthony, Pillar of the Church,
St. Anthony, Worthy Priest of God,
St. Anthony, Apostolic Preacher,
St. Anthony, Teacher of truth,
St. Anthony, Terror of evil spirits,
St. Anthony, Comforter of the afflicted,
St. Anthony, Helper in necessities,
St. Anthony, Deliverer of captives,
St. Anthony, Guide of the erring,
St. Anthony, Restorer of lost things,
St. Anthony, Chosen intercessor,
St. Anthony, Continuous worker of miracles,

pray for us!

Be merciful unto us, *spare us, O Lord!*
Be merciful unto us, *hear us, O Lord!*
From all evil,
From all sin,
From all dangers of body and soul,

118

From the snares of the devil,
From pestilence, famine and war,
From eternal death,
Through the merits of St. Anthony,
Through his zeal for the conversion of sinners,
Through his desire for the crown of martyrdom,
Through his fatigues and labors,
Through his preaching and teaching,
Through his tears of penance,
Through his patience and humility,
Through his glorious death,
Through the number of his wonderful deeds,
In the day of judgment,   *O Lord, deliver us!*
We sinners,
That You bring us to true penance,
That You grant us patience in our trials,
That You assist us in our needs,
That You grant us our petitions,
That You kindle the fire of your love in us,
That You favor us with the protection and
    intercession of St. Anthony,
Son of God,   *we beseech You, hear us!*
Lamb of God, who take away the sins of the world,
    spare us, O Lord!
Lamb of God, who take away the sins of the world,
    graciously hear us, O Lord!
Lamb of God, who take away the sins of the world,
    have mercy on us!
Christ hear us! *Christ graciously hear us.*
V. Pray for us, blessed Anthony:
R. That we may be made worthy of the promises of Christ.

Let us pray:

Almighty and eternal God, You glorified Your
faithful Confessor and Doctor, St. Anthony, with the
gift of working miracles. Graciously grant that what
we seek with confidence through his merits, we may
surely receive through his prayers. Through Christ
our Lord. Amen.